# The White Mile Trial

# The White Mile Trial

## A River Rafting Tragedy and the Courtroom Justice That Followed

Cecil Kuhne

ROWMAN & LITTLEFIELD
Lanham • Boulder • New York • London

Rowman & Littlefield
Bloomsbury Publishing Inc, 1385 Broadway, New York, NY 10018, USA
Bloomsbury Publishing Plc, 50 Bedford Square, London, WC1B 3DP, UK
Bloomsbury Publishing Ireland, 29 Earlsfort Terrace, Dublin 2, D02 AY28, Ireland
www.rowman.com

British Library Cataloguing in Publication Information available

**Library of Congress Cataloging-in-Publication Data**

Names: Kuhne, Cecil C., III, 1952- author.
Title: The white mile trial : a river rafting tragedy and the courtroom justice that
    followed / Cecil Kuhne.
Description: Lanham: Rowman & Littlefield Publishers, 2025. |
    Includes bibliographical references and index.
Identifiers: LCCN 2024032277 | ISBN 9798881802011 (cloth) |
    ISBN 9798881802028 (ebook)
Subjects: LCSH: Thompson, Ron (Rafting guide)—Trials, litigation, etc. | Trials
    (Manslaughter)—British Columbia. | Liability for sports accidents—British
    Columbia. | Rafting (Sports)—British Columbia. | Advertising agencies—
    Law and legislation—United States.
Classification: LCC KE229.T46 K84 2025 | DDC 346.7303/23—dc23/eng/20240916
LC record available at https://lccn.loc.gov/2024032277

For product safety related questions contact productsafety@bloomsbury.com.

*I do not think the forest would be so bright, nor the water so warm, nor love so sweet, if there were no danger in the lakes.*

—C. S. Lewis, *Out of the Silent Planet*[1]

---

# Contents

# Prologue

It was a beautiful, sunny day in the Canadian Rockies, and the cold, emerald green waters of the Chilko River swept briskly by as the 12 men boarded the 18-foot-long inflatable raft. The river was higher than it had been in years. The guide, Ron Thompson, rowed the boat into the current, just as he had done without incident for the past 13 years and, to be precise, 207 trips.

The Chilko River, located 200 miles north of Vancouver, had long been famous for the 15-mile stretch of whitewater in Lava Canyon that some have said was one of the most challenging whitewater runs in North America. In its short span through the canyon, the river drops over 1,500 feet—a dramatic descent by any standard.

Those on board the raft were well aware that downstream lay three renowned rapids—Bidwell, White Kilometer, and White Mile—that churned voraciously and continuously for seven miles. Experiencing this stretch of roiling river was precisely why these 11 men—powerful executives employed by some of the largest corporations in the United States—had traveled from so far away. Among the maelstrom, the series of rapids known as White Mile had an especially well-deserved reputation for enormous reversals and intimidating hydraulics.

With his vast experience on the river, Thompson knew the currents of the Chilko like the back of his hand. On the scale of whitewater difficulty, this stretch of cataracts was typically rated as Class IV, and some would say Class V. It was certainly nothing to be trifled with, but no one had ever drowned on the Chilko.

It was Saturday morning, August 1, 1987. Six members of the group had made the run down Lava Canyon two days earlier, and they quipped that the rough dirt road out of the river was worse than the rapids. The other five men chose instead to fish for the steelhead trout that made the area famous.

This particular raft and fishing excursion into the wilds of Canada was organized by an American marketing executive named Art Wolfe. He saw the trip as a client-development tool on behalf of his employer, DDB Needham, one of the largest advertising agencies in the world. Wolfe was president in the Chicago office, where he directed all U.S. activities for an impressive roster of corporate marketing departments. He had organized a number of rafting trips in the past, viewing them as a productive means of bonding members of the Needham team together with its clients and future prospects.

Those who had signed on for the Canadian adventure were either account executives from Needham or top-level officers from major U.S. corporations—such as Procter & Gamble, Clorox, Kraft, Mattel, and Merrill Lynch. Many of the men had rafted before with Wolfe, and some of them had been on rivers with hazards more extensive and severe than those offered by Lava Canyon.

Less than three hours after they pushed off from shore, five of the passengers—almost half the group—would be dead. No one knows exactly what happened at White Mile, but the bow of the raft caught an errant current, turned abruptly, and then unexpectedly careened into a rock midstream. All but one of the men were dumped into the tortured currents. Six of the swimmers made it to shore and survived. The other five men were swept to their death in the frigid waters of the Chilko River. The deceased unfortunately included the following:

James Fasules
Robert Goldstein
Richard O'Reilly
Stuart Sharpe
Gene Yovetich

Those who managed to survive were the following:

Jack Collins
Earl Madsen
Michael Miles
Joe Morrison
Ron Thompson
Al Wolfe
Arthur Zeikel

Among those who drowned was Robert Goldstein, who was 50 years old and one of the most powerful figures in the marketing world. Goldstein was vice president of advertising at Procter & Gamble, where he supervised a budget of $1.4 billion. He also held leadership positions in a number of national advertising organizations, including the Advertising Council, the American Advertising Federation, the Advertising Educational Foundation, and the International Advertising Association.

Also dead was Richard O'Reilly, 65 years of age, the president of his own advertising firm in Greenwich, Connecticut, which handled the 1980 Reagan campaign. He was currently national director of the Media-Advertising Partnership for a Drug-Free America, a $500-million-per-year project.

Three DDB Needham executives perished on the river that day: Jim Fasules, 63, a former senior vice president, as well as two young senior vice presidents at the agency, Stuart Sharpe, 37, and Gene Yovetich, 41. Of those who were employed by Needham, only Art Wolfe survived.

Ron Thompson, the outfitter, was later said to have remarked, "I just spent 13 years of my life doing something that I felt was a good thing for people and for society in general, and I have to wonder now if it was worth it. My thoughts are entirely with these men. Some of them I knew for years."

After the shock of the tragedy subsided, litigation ensued. The most publicized trial involved a lawsuit filed by Lenore Fasules, the widow of Jim Fasules, the retired Needham executive. Interestingly enough, Mrs. Fasules sued the organizer of the trip, DDB Needham—not Ron Thompson, the outfitter—as the party responsible for the death of her husband. This was undoubtedly an effort to reach the lucrative assets of a large corporate entity in the United States rather than the meager funds of a shoestring company in Canada.

# Chapter One

The bailiff entered the Chicago courtroom and sharply announced to the lawyers, jury members, and spectators gathered there, "All rise. The federal district court for the northern district of Illinois, eastern division, calls to order cause number 89-CV-1078, Lenore F. Fasules, Individually and as Executor of the Estate of James E. Fasules, versus DDB Needham, Worldwide, Inc. and Omnicom Group, Inc., the Honorable Charles P. Kocoras presiding."

The judge, clad in typical black robes, briskly entered the courtroom from a wood-paneled door and took his seat in a tall leather chair behind the bench. He quietly reviewed the documents before him and then announced to the lawyers without even looking up, "Counsel for plaintiff may present his opening."

Brian Crowe rose from the counsel table, and with the confidence of a litigator who felt completely at ease in the courtroom, he approached the jury box to begin his introductory remarks.

Brian Crowe wanted to first introduce the jury to the person of Jim Fasules before his tragic death.

"Ladies and gentlemen, this case is about the corporate world of business. It is about power. It is about an abnormally dangerous activity. It is about negligence, and it is about the tragic loss of a very loved and talented man.

"My name is Brian Crowe, and my partner, Phillip Goldberg, and I represent Lenore Fasules, the widow of Jim Fasules, the deceased. I suppose I should start in June of 1948 because those were good days in the life of Jim Fasules. He was 24 years old. He was recently graduated from the University of Valparaiso. He had been accepted at the University of Chicago in their marketing program. But more importantly, his girlfriend of several years, Lenore, had accepted his proposal of marriage.

"The evidence will show that Jim and Lenore were married for 39 years. They had three children: Jim, who is a pediatric cardiologist in Arkansas; Gary, who followed his dad's footsteps and is a businessman; and Nancy, who is a freelance lyricist living in California. I believe the evidence will show that this was a loving, caring family.

"Jim's career was a marvelous one. Shortly after Jim graduated from the University of Chicago he accepted a position with Needham, which is today called DDB Needham Worldwide, and it is the defendant in this case. It is the fifteenth largest advertising company in the world. Jim Fasules's career skyrocketed with Needham due to his energy, hard work, and a love of people. Jim was responsible for the accounts of famous companies: Wrigley Gum, Campbell Soup, Johnson Wax.

"The evidence is going to show that Jim Fasules's knowledge of the advertising business was enormous and that his willingness to share that knowledge with young men and women was limitless. Jim was very fortunate, and when he was 59 years old, he retired, and it was a retirement of dreams. Jim and his wife Lenore did the things that they had always dreamed about. They bird-watched. They hiked. They went and looked at antiques. They collected American folk art. But most importantly, they were able to do what they loved all their life—they went fishing.

"They loved fishing so much that they purchased a trailer in Ennis, Montana. It was a small trailer, and they could fish in the clear waters of Montana. Jim was a fisherman, not a risk taker, but his dream retirement would end, and it was very, very short-lived.

"In 1987, Jim was 63 years old. On July 27, 1987, Jim and Lenore received a phone call at their trailer in Montana, and it was the beginning of the destruction of their dreams. That phone call came from a man named Al Wolfe, who was the president of the United States division of DDB Needham Worldwide. Al Wolfe was a different kind of business executive than Jim Fasules was.

"Jim Fasules loved to teach advertising. He taught at the University of Nevada at Reno and was offered a permanent position shortly before his death. Al Wolfe, on the other hand, developed client relationships through power and what we now call macho. He was indeed a macho man, and it goes way back.

"Al Wolfe in the late '60s would plan hunting trips, but not ordinary hunting trips. He would take business executives and advertising people to hunt elk and deer in wilderness areas where they would have to sleep in tents. They loved it, and that's the way Wolfe developed power. In time, the hunting wasn't enough. Wolfe developed a new kind of adventure. His fancies turned to whitewater rafting—not ordinary whitewater rafting, but rafting on the most dangerous rivers in North America."

Brian Crowe continued with his opening remarks, in particular the river and rapids that killed Jim Fasules.

"Ladies and gentlemen, I believe the evidence is going to show that whitewater rapids are classified by an international scale that ranges from Class I to Class VI. Class V rapids are long and very violent rapids with highly congested routes, and they must first be scouted from shore. Rescue conditions are difficult, and there are significant hazards to life in the event of a mishap.

"Let's talk for a moment about the Class V river in this case. It is the Chilko River in British Columbia. The Chilko River is indeed a Class V river, and it is one of the most dangerous rivers on the continent of North America.

"Witnesses will tell you that at the beginning of the rapids on the Chilko River, the river drops 1,500 feet in 15 miles. As you enter the mouth of these rapids, the river narrows. It constricts, and sharp rock walls rise. The river then drops into a deep canyon, and in that canyon are three rapids—Bidwell Rapid, White Kilometer Rapid, and White Mile Rapid. These are three continuous rapids over almost seven miles. Witnesses in this case will tell you that the waves of those rapids are as much as six feet high, and the sound is like a freight train going through a tunnel.

"The Chilko River is a Class V river. This was Al Wolfe's game, and he has quite a history. In the early and mid-'70s, he took corporate executive and advertising people on the Selway River in Idaho. It has Class IV and Class V rapids. He took two of those trips: one in the early '70s and one in the mid-'70s. The evidence will show that it got boring for him. So he looked for more exciting rivers, and he went to the Salmon River in Idaho, and it turned out it was a Class III river and really boring. So in 1983, he went back to the Class IV rapids of the Selway.

"In 1985, he took his first trip down the Chilko River. In fact, he knew how dangerous the Chilko was because he hired a helicopter and flew over it before he booked the trip. Al Wolfe knew the dangers of the Chilko, and what is worse, he knew the precautions that had to be taken—precautions like two rafts and precautions like never having more than six to eight people in a raft. He knew the dangers. He knew the precautions."

Brian Crowe stopped for a moment and then walked over to counsel's table to retrieve a yellow legal pad with handwritten notes. His next emphasis would be the responsibility of the Needham corporation for the death of Jim Fasules.

"Ladies and gentlemen, make no mistake about it. These were business trips. The evidence is going to show that in 1985 and in 1987 it was Al Wolfe, the president acting on behalf of the Needham corporation, who handpicked Ron Thompson, the guide. You are going to hear a lot about Ron Thompson. He is the guide who was involved in the fatal 1987 tragedy.

"On the 1987 trip, Wolfe planned and organized the rafting trip on the Chilko. Wolfe selected the individuals to be invited, and Needham paid for the food, the lodging, and the services of the river guide for each of the participants on the trip. Check request forms were filled out by Wolfe or his secretary and submitted to Needham for payment of those expenses. All of the expenses for the Needham employees who participated in the trip were deducted by the defendant for income tax purposes as new business expenses.

"Let's take a look and see who was invited on this trip: Jack Collins, president of Clorox; Bill Connell, an executive of Procter & Gamble; Bob Goldstein, an executive director of Procter & Gamble; Bill Korn, president of Frito-Lay; Robert Lackovic, vice president and director of marketing of the First Nationwide Banks; Earl Madsen, he was an attorney in private practice and went to college with Al Wolfe; Jack MacDonough, vice president and manager of Anheuser-Busch; Pat McGinnis, director of Ralston Purina, the pet food division; Mike Miles, president of Kraft Foods; Joe Morrison, an executive with Mattel Toys; Pat Mulcahy, president or chairman of the EverReady Division of Ralston Purina; Dick O'Reilly, Advertising Partnership for a Drug-Free America and the American Association of Advertising Agents; Alan

Pando, president of DDB Needham-West; Philip Reiss, senior partner of Davis & Gilbert in New York, who represents Omnicom, which is a parent corporation of Needham; Gene Yovetich, an executive of DDB Needham; and Arthur Zeikel, an executive of Merrill Lynch.

"Sixteen of those 17 people are either existing or former business prospects and clients of DDB Needham. And yet the defendant says that this was not a business trip as to Jim Fasules. The evidence is going to show that Jim Fasules in fact did some consulting business for Needham after he was retired. The evidence is going to show that Mr. Fasules worked on the Kraft account at one time with executive Mike Miles, who was invited on the trip. And above all, Jim Fasules knew the language and had the knowledge of consumer products that all of these executives' companies dealt in. There is no doubt that Jim Fasules was brought along for a business reason. But it is important for the defendant to deny it in this case, and so they will.

"Shortly before July 27, 1987, when that fatal phone call came, there had been a cancellation, and one of these executives dropped out. There was a brief conversation between Wolfe in his corporate office in Chicago and Fasules in his trailer in Montana. Believe me it was a brief conversation. And there will be disputes as to what was said.

"After that phone conversation, Jim turned to Lenore and said, 'Lenore, I always wanted to go up there in British Columbia because the place is famous for steelhead trout.' She said, 'So go.' And he called his son, Gary, and he spoke to him for a long time about fishing. Not one word to Lenore, not one word to Gary about whitewater rafting.

"I submit that after you have heard the evidence in this case, you aren't going to know what was said on that phone conversation. But you will know this for sure—that Wolfe never, ever told Jim Fasules about Class IV and Class V rapids and the dangers inherent in those rapids. And Wolfe never told Jim that all of these men who went on this trip would have to raft down the Chilko River on the last day to get on the plane to go home. These things he never said.

"After that phone conversation Jim Fasules decided to go fishing in British Columbia and he left. He never returned to Montana again. He got on that plane and flew to Vancouver. The men who you will hear about in the next couple of weeks met in Vancouver on the evening of July 29: Jack Collins, Bob Goldstein, Earl Madsen, Mike Miles, Joe

Morrison, Dick O'Reilly, Gene Yovetich, Arthur Zeikel, Stuart Sharpe, and Jim Fasules.

"The men got on small planes in Vancouver and took off for the interior of British Columbia. The planes flew over dense forests and mountains covered with snow. And eventually they landed in this wilderness area on an airstrip that is described as nothing more than a rocky path cut out from the mountain. That night all of the men stayed at a Chilko Lake Lodge. There were other people there, other visitors to the wilderness area. Germans were there, other people were in the lodge. The Needham men all stayed in cabins."

Crowe straightened his jacket and continued the story, closely observing the jury as he tried to get a read on their reactions. Now he would talk about the accident itself.

"The next morning they all got up. Our witness is going to tell you what it was like when they got up. Because he had met Ron Thompson, Wolfe's handpicked guide. And here is what our witness says. He says that he was surprised about the confusing and haphazard way the equipment was thrown on the ground. He says, 'Thompson was a laid-back, disorganized, casual, non–decision maker who stood out like a sore thumb when compared to the organized, aggressive personalities of the group.'

"I believe the evidence is going to show that it was Thompson's non–decision-making personality in response to Wolfe's aggressive personality in demanding privacy of his group that led to Jim Fasules's death.

"That day the fishermen separated from the group. Those that wanted to go fishing did. And those that chose to go fishing were Jim Fasules, Joe Morrison, Arthur Zeikel, Bob Goldstein, and Jack Collins. They all went, and Fasules especially, to do the thing they had gone to the Chilko area for—to fish for steelhead. The other men, Wolfe, Sharpe—who worked for Wolfe—Gene Yovetich—who worked for Wolfe—O'Reilly, Miles, and Zeikel got in a van and drove an hour and a half farther into the wilderness to go whitewater rafting down Lava Canyon.

"When they got to the shores of the put-in point, Ron Thompson, the guide, the casual non–decision maker, wanted to take two rafts. Why two rafts? Because if people fall out of one raft and are drowning, the people in the other raft can pick them up out of the water.

"In fact, John McAlpine, his employee, will testify in a videotape in this trial that he prefers two rafts because if a person falls out of one raft, those in the other boat can pick him out of water.

"But do you know what happened, ladies and gentlemen? The evidence is going to show that Ron Thompson, Wolfe's handpicked guy, asks Wolfe's permission to go down the river with another group behind them so it will be safe. Al Wolfe made it quite clear to Thompson that the Needham men were going to stay separate and that no other group would be with them.

"What happened? Wolfe called the shots, and Thompson obeyed, and that other boat went down the Chilko River with John McAlpine at the oars. And Thompson, dutifully obeying, took the Needham people in another raft far away from that other group.

"On Thursday those six men went down the Chilko River, and you know they were lucky—they made it. But of those six men, Zeikel, Sharpe, and O'Reilly would only have 48 hours to live."

Crowe was weaving a powerful narrative, and he sensed that the jury was anticipating what would happen next to the 12 men on the river.

"Friday morning they all got up. It had rained all Thursday night, and it rained real hard Friday, and more water fell into the Chilko River. The men were cold and damp, and they were talking about going home or going back to the Chilko Lodge. For some reason they didn't, and they went farther downstream, and they camped once again.

"That Saturday morning it was bright and it was sunny. All the suitcases and fishing equipment were put in the vans, and one van drove away leaving Thompson and the 11 men at the campsite. Another van pulled up with John McAlpine behind the wheel, but you knew he wasn't going to stay because in the van were some non-Needham people. The van with the non-Needham people had another raft behind it, and it drove away.

"The eleven men and Thompson went to the banks of the Chilko River, and what was waiting for them on the shore? You know it. One raft for all 11 men and Thompson. One raft.

"Ladies and gentlemen, John McAlpine, Thompson's employee, is going to testify that Al Wolfe put pressure on Ron Thompson to go down in that single raft. The men got in the raft, and they began a slow float—90 minutes' worth—to the mouth of Bidwell Rapids.

"I hate to interrupt the story at this point, but I have to tell you that the lack of two rafts wasn't the only thing wrong with this trip. It wasn't the only negligent thing that happened before this raft entered an inherently dangerous activity. There were other things wrong.

"An expert witness, Les Bechdel, who's probably one of the leading authorities on the subject of whitewater safety in North America, will testify to the other things. You will hear his testimony. The evidence is going to show that in addition to a lack of two rafts, Thompson and Wolfe failed to warn Jim Fasules and the others of the dangers of the Chilko and of their slim chances of survival if they fell into the river in Lava Canyon. The 12 men in the raft caused it to be overcrowded, making it less maneuverable for the trip down the rapids, and Al Wolfe was also aware of this.

"Les Bechdel will testify, ladies and gentlemen, that he had never been on a trip before where there were more than six or eight people per raft. The evidence is going to show that Thompson didn't provide dry suits or wetsuits to protect the men from the effects of the cold water in the event that someone fell overboard and to provide additional buoyancy and protection against sharp rocks.

"The evidence will show that Thompson failed to give adequate safety instructions about what to do to save themselves and each other should they fall in the water. The evidence will show that Thompson failed to instruct the passengers before the trip that if they should hit a rock, they were supposed to 'high-side' to prevent the raft from flipping. In other words, they were to get to the front of the raft and straighten it out.

"The evidence will show that Thompson failed to provide three throw ropes—one in the front, one in the rear, and one to the oarsman—to save a drowning rafter. The evidence will show that Thompson failed to provide safety helmets to protect a swimmer from striking his head and face against a rock and to increase his abilities to survive in the water.

"The evidence will show that Thompson failed to scout the river after the heavy rains fell all day Thursday and all day Friday. Bechdel will testify that Thompson not only failed to have more than one raft, but he failed to have a safety kayak accompanying the group.

"The evidence will show that Thompson failed to have people standing on shore at given points along the rapids with throw ropes to save those that might fall in the water.

"Finally, both Thompson and Wolfe were negligent in their selection of the Lava Canyon of the Chilko River as the spot to take Jim Fasules, given his age of 63 years and his lack of experience.

"The evidence will show that for 90 minutes the raft floated down the relatively calm waters of the Chilko River, the place where the steelhead had abounded in those calm waters. There were a few minor ripples. The men got somewhat wet.

"Finally they got to Bidwell Rapids. You couldn't see the rapids yet. They pulled out of the water. The raft had a slow leak, and they were going to pump it up. At the point before the raft entered Bidwell there is no way that it can be said, as these defendants are going to urge upon you, that the risk was open and obvious to Jim Fasules. He had never seen the Chilko rapids. He had never seen the river before this moment.

"The evidence is going to show that Jim Fasules had been rafting once in his life. He had been fishing up in Montana on the Madison River, and the raft went through some momentary Class III rapids which required him to take his line out of the water.

"Les Bechdel, the expert, is going to testify that this experience could in no way prepare one for the risks that were involved in the Class IV and Class V rapids of the Chilko River."

Crowe hesitated briefly, just for dramatic effect. He knew not to rush the moment.

"The men are at Bidwell. They don't see the rapids yet. Because some of the men are wet, they change places. The only man who stays in front is Wolfe. He has got to make sure he stays in front. Madsen, O'Reilly, Fasules, and Yovetich are in the front, and the others are in the back. The raft then begins its descent down Bidwell.

"Evidence will be produced in this trial to tell you that that was a violent ride. Thompson the guide will tell you that Jim Fasules looked frightened. He could tell by his body position. Thompson will tell you how inexperienced all these other middle-aged executives were as they leaned back away from the rushing water as they bumped into Thompson as he tried to row the boat.

"And yet, after they finished the Bidwell Rapids and before they entered the White Kilometer, there is a flat stretch of water. Does Thompson invite Fasules to get out? Of course not. How could he? Remember where we are. We are in the middle of Lava Canyon, where there are lava formations going up a hundred feet through rock and debris in a wilderness area. And they continued into White Kilometer, another violent ride, and then finally they reached White Mile.

"When they were 200 yards into White Mile, suddenly protruding out of the water is a large flat rock to the left. Because there were so many men in that boat, Thompson could not maneuver it. The raft was so heavy that it punched through the pillow or cushion that is usually in front of a rock and pushes a raft away, and the raft punched right through it and went up on the rock. And only after the raft hits the rock does Thompson yell, 'High side!' and now it is too late.

"At White Mile 11 of those 12 men fell into the cold, violent waters of the Chilko River. Only one man was able to stay in the boat, and that is Jack Collins. And for Jack Collins, I submit to you the sight was terrible. He will tell you how he saw Jim Fasules in the water and Jim was looking at him with eyes filled with anger. Collins later sees Jim again, and Jim is looking at him. It is his testimony that 'Jim Fasules's lips were moving and his eyes were imploring me and he seemed to be saying to me, "Help me, help."'

"And what does Collins do? He tries to help Jim, but not with a rope because there aren't any ropes left in the raft. Thompson had grabbed the only one when he fell out of the raft. And you know it wouldn't matter because nobody told Collins how to use a throw rope anyway.

"So Collins grabs a hold of Fasules by his life jacket, and because he sees he is pulling his life jacket off of him and he is fearful that he is going to strip him of his life jacket, Collins lets him go.

"The evidence will show that Jim Fasules was carried down the stream of the whitewater and would eventually drown and die of other contributing causes.

"Suddenly, Earl Madsen grabs the raft. Earl Madsen hangs on to the raft, Collins reaches in with his hand to try to pull him up, but he doesn't have the strength to do it, and he doesn't have a rope to help him. And the weight of Madsen's body is holding down the raft like a sea anchor, and the other men begin to float down the river.

"The evidence will show that Thompson, Zeikel, and Miles were able to quickly get out of the water. They were very fortunate. The other men—other than Madsen and Collins—floated down the river.

"All of them—save Al Wolfe—would die. Al Wolfe lived. He had a cut on his knee. Those other five men—O'Reilly, Sharpe, Gene

Yovetich, Jim Fasules, Bob Goldstein—the coroner is going to tell you that each and every one of them drowned and died of contributing causes.

"Collins and Madsen lived. And the evidence, ladies and gentlemen, is dramatic. That eventually Collins was able to pull that raft over to shore, tie it up, and Madsen got out of the water. His body was shaking from hypothermia. The men hugged each other until Madsen stopped shaking, and then they began to look for some form of civilization. So remote was that area that it was five hours before they are spotted by a rescue helicopter.

"The evidence will show that rescue helicopters and boats took almost a day and a half before they found all of the bodies, and some had to be lifted out because it was that remote.

"Thompson—a man in good physical condition—it took him almost two and a half to three hours to get himself to the Taseko junction, the take-out point where those planes were supposed to be, and he told his girlfriend Stephanie Miller to call the Royal Canadian Mounted Police. The Mounties were assigned to the case. Constable Wiltshire, who will testify during this trial, will tell you how they went in and found the bodies.

"The evidence will show that the body of Stuart Sharpe was found over here [indicating] at Point A. The body of Richard O'Reilly was found here at Point B. The body of Gene Yovetich was found over here, 20 to 25 miles away from the Chilko River. The body of James Fasules, my client, was found over in Blue Canyon, 20 to 25 miles away. The body of Robert Goldstein was found amongst some logs and debris over here, perhaps five or six miles from the site. I won't bore you with those details. Constable Wiltshire will come and tell you."

The skilled advocate that he was, Brian Crowe had reached the apex of his narrative. He knew it was time to start winding down.

"Ladies and gentlemen, the evidence is going to show in this case— and I can tell you in conclusion—that this tragedy resulted in several things, which you will be asked about at the end of this case and which you will have to decide.

"I believe that the evidence will show, first of all, that this was a dangerous whitewater rafting trip and that it was a business venture sponsored by DOB Needham, through its president and agent, Al

Wolfe. Two, I believe the evidence is going to show that Fasules was a business invitee on the trip. Three, that Needham, through Al Wolfe, was negligent in the organization and operation of that trip in hiring Thompson. Four, that the rafting trip through Lava Canyon was inherently an abnormally dangerous activity. Five, that Ron Thompson was negligent in the organization and operation of the trip—no warnings, poor instructions, lack of two rafts and a safety kayak, inadequate throw ropes and no wetsuits, no helmets—and that DDB Needham is responsible for Thompson's negligent conduct.

"The evidence will show that Jim Fasules did not assume the risk of those things that caused his death, and the evidence will show that as a proximate result of the wrongful acts of Needham, through its agents Al Wolfe and Ron Thompson, that Jim Fasules died on August 1, 1987.

"The evidence will show that after this incident Thompson shut down his rafting business on the Chilko River and would do some farming and other minor rafting, but not on the Chilko.

"The evidence will show that Al Wolfe, the president of DB Needham, one year later flew halfway across the world and rafted the Yangtze River in China, the most dangerous rapids in the world.

"Lenore Fasules survived, as have her children. I believe the evidence is going to show that she suffered losses, that she suffered the loss of services and society of her husband. I believe the evidence is going to show that Jim and Nancy and Gary suffered the loss of services and society of dad. And I believe the evidence is going to show that Lenore and the children suffered economic loss. And finally, I believe the evidence is going to show that Jim Fasules suffered conscientious pain and suffering before his death.

"Ladies and gentlemen, when this case is all done, when we are given a chance at closing argument, I am going to ask that you return a verdict in favor of my clients and against the defendant DOB Needham on all of the elements of damages that we will able to prove to you.

"We thank you for your time and your attention."

# Chapter Two

Al Wolfe was clearly a mover and shaker in the busy Chicago office of DDB Needham Worldwide, one of the largest advertising companies in the world. As he scurried about the corridors of the agency, Wolfe managed the company's U.S. division, a formidable position, and his corporate clients included such high flyers as Anheuser-Busch, The Clorox Company, Frito-Lay, General Mills, Nestlé, Procter & Gamble, and Ralston Purina, among many others.

Soft-spoken but straightforward, Wolfe had grown up in Wyoming and was an avid outdoorsman. He had organized adventure-travel trips for his clients and prospects for 20 years. Most of these excursions involved hunting before he moved on to whitewater rafting. In recent years, Wolfe had taken corporate executives down the renowned rapids of the Selway River and the Middle Fork of the Salmon, both located in Idaho and considered two of the most dangerous whitewater rivers in North America. In 1985, Wolfe took a group down the Chilko River in British Columbia without incident, and he planned to do it again in late July 1987.

Wolfe believed that these trips made good business sense because they allowed the executives at DDB Needham and their corporate prospects to flee the pretense and artificiality of the city and escape to the raw beauty of the wilderness, where they could get to know each other and form lasting personal bonds that would translate into solid business relations.

The core group of account executives at DDB Needham traced its roots back to the New York office of Wells Rich Greene, where Wolfe was in charge of the lucrative Procter & Gamble account. How ironic that these men working together in the 1970s promoting Procter &

13

Gamble products (like Sure antiperspirant and Gleem toothpaste) would later share a sad and lasting fate on the Chilko River. At that time Dick O'Reilly—who would drown at White Mile—was a Needham executive handling the day-to-day activities of the P&G account. O'Reilly would go on to become the head of advertising for Ronald Reagan's campaign in 1980 and director of the Advertising Partnership for a Drug-Free America. While he was at Needham, O'Reilly was assisted by a young employee named Joe Morrison, who survived the tragedy on the Chilko River. Morrison would later credit O'Reilly as the mentor who gave him the break he needed to move to Mattel, where he became executive vice president of marketing.

Working for P&G at the time that O'Reilly and Morrison were handling the account were Bob Goldstein and Jack Collins. Bob Goldstein later became vice president of advertising for P&G before he died on the Chilko. Jack Collins had moved to The Clorox Company, where he rose to the position of president and chief executive officer, and he was the only person to remain inside the raft on that unforgettable journey.

Three Needham executives drowned that day on the river: Jim Fasules, Stuart Sharpe, and Gene Yovetich. Fasules was retired from the company, and Sharpe and Yovetich were coheads of the company's account management department. Art Wolfe had strategically included them on the trip because of their relationships with clients who were invited on the trip. Fasules had worked on the Kraft account. Sharpe handled the Clorox account, and Yovetich had previously supervised the Kraft account.

A number of new business prospects were invited on the Chilko trip. Mike Miles was president and chief operating officer of Kraft, a former client of Needham and now a future target. Other prospects included Joe Morrison, vice president of marketing for Mattel Toys, and Arthur Zeikel, president of Merrill Lynch Asset Management.

Many of the men on the Chilko had previously gone rafting on trips organized by Wolfe. Wolfe's rafting trip on Idaho's Selway River in June 1983 included Jack Collins (Clorox), Bob Goldstein (Procter & Gamble), and Joe Morrison (Mattel). The trip down the Chilko in 1985 consisted of Earl Madsen (a lawyer from Colorado and personal friend of Wolfe), Joe Morrison (Mattel), Dick O'Reilly (a consultant in the advertising business), and Arthur Zeikel (Merrill Lynch).

In his initial search for an outfitter on the Chilko, Wolfe chose Ron Thompson, who seemed like a natural fit since he had navigated the Chilko more than 200 times without incident and had been in the outfitting business for 13 years. He came highly recommended by Sobek, a well-respected adventure-travel consolidator, and Jack Currey, the rafting company that Wolfe had used on both the Selway and the Middle Fork of the Salmon.

Wolfe was nothing if not meticulous. Performing due diligence, Wolfe traveled to British Columbia to interview Thompson in person, and the two of them chartered a plane and flew over Lava Canyon, taking close note of the steep drops on the Chilko, including those of White Mile. Wolfe specifically asked Thompson if he had ever had an accident, and Thompson confirmed that he had not. In fact, Thompson said that he had never even capsized on the river. Wolfe was convinced that Thompson was an exceptional guide, and after he returned to Chicago, he proceeded to arrange the trip.

The float down the Chilko in the summer of 1985 went off without a hitch, and all the participants marveled at the magnificent scenery and immensity of the rapids. Wolfe wanted to arrange another raft two years later, and after surveying several options, he decided to return to the Chilko.

The initial itinerary for the group was set:

- Wednesday, July 29: Meet in Vancouver that evening and take charter flights to Chilko Lake.
- Thursday, July 30: Choice of fishing or whitewater rafting.
- Friday, July 31: Choice of fishing or whitewater rafting.
- Saturday, August 1: Whitewater rafting in Lava Canyon and return to Vancouver that evening on charter flights.

In his dealings with Thompson, Wolfe made it clear that he wanted only Needham invitees included in the group. He had been on other rafting trips where strangers had been included, and the resulting incompatibility had made for some awkward and unpleasant experiences. Thompson got the message loud and clear.

Wolfe initially invited 16 men to join the journey. It was largely a group of high-level executives, and most of them were either existing or former clients or business prospects of the agency. Nine of the initial

16 invitees were not interested, unavailable, or later canceled, and three others were eventually added, making a total of 10. Wolfe's final list consisted of the following 11 individuals:

• Jack Collins (Clorox)
• Jim Fasules (retired executive at Needham) who filled in at the last minute when Phil Reiss became unavailable
• Bob Goldstein (Procter & Gamble)
• Earl Madsen (attorney and friend)
• Mike Miles (Kraft)
• Joe Morrison (Mattel)
• Dick O'Reilly (advertising consultant)
• Stuart Sharpe (Needham)
• Gene Yovetich (Needham)
• Arthur Zeikel (Merrill Lynch)

On March 24, Wolfe sent a letter on Needham stationery to all of the invitees describing the agenda: "I have worked out a schedule with Ron Thompson, the outfitter, that provides for fishing or whitewater rafting on the first two days depending on an individual's choice and a third day of whitewater rafting for everyone."

A little over three months later—on July 7—Wolf sent another letter in which he quipped, "Dear fellow Masochist: I think Iwo Jima was retaken with less equipment." The plans had changed somewhat: "We will leave Chilko Lodge for three days and two nights on the Chilko River for various combinations of fishing and rafting as each individual chooses. Tents, sleeping bags, pads, and ground covers will be provided, if any of you have back problems."

On July 27—just two days before the trip was to depart—Phil Reiss, an attorney and longtime friend of Wolfe, had to drop out. Looking for a replacement, Wolfe picked up the phone and called trip member Gene Yovetich, a senior vice president at Needham who had a second home in Montana and who was visiting Jim Fasules, a retired Needham executive, at his second home (actually a trailer house) in Montana.

Did Yovetich think that Jim Fasules, an enthusiastic fly fisherman, would like to go to the Chilko? Fasules was 63 years old and had done some consulting business for Needham after he retired. Wolfe said to Yovetich, "Gene, we have got an opening. Do you think Jim would like to go with us?" Yovetich responded, "Are you kidding? He would love to go. Let me talk to him."

After Yovetich extended the invitation, Fasules turned to his wife Lenore and said, "Lenore, I always wanted to go up there in British Columbia because the place is famous for steelhead trout." She replied, "So go."

An hour later, Fasules called Wolfe and asked, "Al, have you still got an opening on that trip?" When Wolfe confirmed that he did, Fasules said, "You bet. I would love to." Wolfe replied, "Talk to Gene Yovetich, and he will fill you in on the trip, and then we will go from there."

Very little was said about rafting on the Chilko other than Wolfe's brief promise: "I can tell you that there will be great steelhead trout, and there will be 45 minutes of the wildest, woolliest whitewater that you have ever experienced or seen in your life."

Wolfe felt that Fasules would be a good fit for the trip because he had previously worked on the Kraft account, and Kraft executive Mike Miles was joining the trip. Fasules also clearly knew the advertising world of consumer products, and he would easily relate to the other executives.

Needham agreed to cover the expenses of the trip for all the invitees. All they had to do was pay their way to Vancouver. The three executives from Needham—Art Wolfe, Stuart Sharpe, and Gene Yovetich—flew first class to Canada for the trip.

# Chapter Three

After a brief lunch recess, the court in the trial of *Fasules v. D.D.B. Needham Worldwide, Inc.* reconvened for its afternoon session. Judge Korocas had motioned to Bill Swindal, another well-known practitioner among the white-shoe firms of the Chicago bar, that he could begin his opening statement for the defendant.

Bill Swindal gathered his notes and walked toward the jury. Swindal's first and primary job was to defuse the effective opening statement of Brian Crowe.

"Good afternoon, ladies and gentlemen. On Sunday I was half watching the Bears game—and half looking through all of the documents that Mr. Crowe is going to bring here during the trial—and my 12-year-old son turned to me and said, 'Dad, what is this case all about?'

"And my mind immediately went to legal theories and evidence and documents and what the evidence was going to show, and I said, 'This is a case about a man named James Fasules, who made a decision to go fishing and whitewater rafting with some of his friends. After he drowned in a tragic and unforeseen accident, his family is here seeking to hold somebody else responsible for the decisions he made.'

"When someone dies, it is natural to feel sympathy—a true, deep sense of loss. Anger and frustration are also strong emotions when someone dies.

"Ladies and gentlemen, we are not here to prove or to determine if Jim Fasules was a good man, was a good father, was good husband, or was a good grandfather. Because he was. As the court told you when he instructed you at the beginning of the case, sympathy and emotion do not have any place in this trial. Trial by jury is a unique system in the world. We are blessed in this country to have this system. It makes

19

us different, and it is an awesome task that we place on ourselves as citizens to sit in judgment of our fellow citizens.

"The court will give you tools to help you in your deliberations during this trial when you have heard the evidence. The judge will make rulings during the course of the trial on the evidence—what evidence is in and what evidence you should not hear. Perhaps it is inappropriate under the law, and perhaps it is unfair or too prejudicial. At the end of the case, the court will also give you instructions on what the law is.

"What you brought with you today are tools that will help you in deciding the facts in this case—your common sense, your own understanding, and knowledge of the ordinary affairs of life—and with those tools and having heard the evidence, you will be able to separate the true facts from the fiction and fantasy of the argument."

Swindal then introduced the jury to the other members of the trip.

"I am Bill Swindal, and together with my partner Debra Davy, we represent a big corporation called DOB Needham Worldwide, Inc. Like any other corporation, it only acts through people. In this case, they were represented by Al Wolfe, who at the time of the events was 55 years of age and was the president of DOB Needham, based here in Chicago. You will be asked to decide in this trial whether Al Wolfe did something wrong that caused the death of James Fasules.

"Who is Jim Fasules? Mr. Crowe has spent a good period of time explaining to you who Jim Fasules was. Briefly, the evidence will show that he retired from DOB Needham as senior vice president. He was an outdoorsman. He was an avid fisherman. He hiked. He had his place in Montana.

"Who else was on this trip? Let me show you pictures of the men who were there. This is Al Wolfe. This gentleman here is Earl Madsen. Earl Madsen is a lawyer. His office and his firm are in Boulder, Colorado, right outside Denver. Al Wolfe and Earl Madsen have been friends for years. They both went to the University of Wyoming. They served on various committees for the University of Wyoming. Al Wolfe and DOB Needham do work for Budweiser. Earl Madsen and his law firm do work for Coors. There has never been a business relationship between Earl Madsen and Al Wolfe. There couldn't be.

"This gentleman is Mike Miles. He is the chairman at Kraft located right up the street here in Glenview. Mike Miles had known Al Wolfe for many years because Miles used to be with the Leo Burnett Advertising Agency, a competitor of Al Wolfe. At the time of this accident, Kraft was not doing business with DDB Needham. They had been fired years ago.

"This is Dick O'Reilly. Dick O'Reilly was in advertising. He was very instrumental in the campaign of Ronald Reagan. The evidence will also show he was involved in an organization called Partnership for a Drug-Free America. I am sure you have seen the commercial on television—the picture of the frying pan with the egg in it and the narrator saying, 'This is your mind, this is your mind on drugs.'

"This gentleman is Jack Collins. At the time of this accident, he was the president of Clorox. He, too, had been a longtime friend of Al Wolfe, and at the time of the accident, Clorox was a client of DDB Needham. Al Wolfe had met Jack Collins years ago when Jack Collins worked for Procter & Gamble, which is where Bob Goldstein worked. Bob Goldstein was a longtime friend of Al Wolfe. DDB Needham did not do business with Procter & Gamble.

"This gentleman with the beard is Joe Morrison. Al Wolfe had hired Joe Morrison to work for him early in his career, and Joe had left the advertising agency and gone to work for Mattel Toys, and that is where he was at the time of this accident. Mattel wasn't a client of DDB Needham either.

"This is James Fasules, the man with the mustache and the white golfing hat. This gentleman with the Frito-Lay hat—that is Stu Sharpe, one of the vice presidents of DDB Needham at the time.

"The last picture I will show you is Art Zeikel, who was the president of Merrill Lynch Asset Management at the time of the accident. And Art Zeikel came on the trip because he was a good friend of Dick O'Reilly. The evidence will be that Dick O'Reilly had asked Al Wolfe if he could bring a friend along, and that was Art Zeikel.

"The other gentleman in this picture that is Ron Thompson. The dark-haired young man next to him is his employee, John McAlpine.

"Now, Jim Fasules, like all of the other men on this trip, was a knowledgeable, sophisticated, educated man who was used to making decisions in his life and stood up for the decisions that he made. That is what the evidence will show, ladies and gentlemen."

Swindal had done his best to humanize the members of the Chilko trip so that the jury would forget that the defendant was a large, impersonal, multinational corporation. Swindal also wanted to convey the competence with which the raft trip was planned and the safety record of the outfitter who conducted the trip.

"Let's talk about Ron Thompson, who will testify in this case, and he will tell you that he was in charge of this trip and that he was responsible for going through the Lava Canyon section of Chilko River and no one else. He and he alone made the decision of when to raft and how to raft. He will sit in the witness stand, and he will tell you that.

"How did Al Wolfe find Ron Thompson? In 1985, prior to going to the Chilko River for the first time, Al Wolfe had called a river guide he had used in the past. His name was Steve Curry. Wolfe will tell you during the course of the trial that he told Steve Curry he was looking for another river to go rafting on and was looking for a good guide, someone that was as good as Steve Curry. Steve Curry recommended Ron Thompson. Al went then to an organization called Sobek, which is one of the largest adventure travel brokers in the United States. They recommended Ron Thompson and Thompson Guiding for trips on the Chilko River.

"Al called Ron. He flew up there and he talked to him. Wolfe said he got on the plane, and he looked at the river. The group went on the '85 trip without incident. You will also hear evidence in this case that Ron Thompson had over 13 years of experience running the Chilko River. He had over 200 trips through Lava Canyon without incident.

"The evidence will also show that there were several commercial rafting companies in British Columbia doing the Chilko River. One of them was called Hyak. And its owner at the time, Jim Lavalley, will be here to tell you how they ran the Chilko River.

"The evidence will show that the Chilko River through Lava Canyon is good whitewater. It is not inherently or abnormally dangerous. The evidence will show that several companies did it on a repeated basis for many years. This is the first death on the Chilko River, and it occurred on August 1, 1987.

"Jack Collins, Earl Madsen, Al Wolfe, Ron Thompson, and John McAlpine all were in Lava Canyon that day. They will all testify in this case. And they will all tell you that Ron Thompson ran that trip—not Al Wolfe. There is a difference between an organizer and the guide. There is no dispute in this case that Al Wolfe organized this trip. There never has been a dispute in this case about that.

"But the evidence will show that an organizer has a different role, if you will. The organizer, the evidence will show, is a person who organizes a chartered trip and takes care of the logistics. The organizer gets the people to the point where the professional takes over. The outfitter, on the other hand, when running the rafting trip through the river, is like the captain of the ship.

"Now, you have heard a lot about the Chilko River, and you are going to hear a lot more. And to set the scene for you, ladies and gentlemen, I am going to show you at this time what is already in evidence, a short video of the Chilko River. The video itself has a lot of helicopter noise because it was taken the day after the accident. And on the helicopter were Constable Wiltshire, who will testify tomorrow, and Ron Thompson. And they are going over the Lava Canyon section of the Chilko River. On the river, you will see a raft, and in the raft is John McAlpine. What John McAlpine was doing in that raft that day was riding down the Chilko River to retrieve the raft that had been in the accident the day before.

"That, ladies and gentlemen, is the section of Lava Canyon on the Chilko River. Several companies commercially whitewater rafted in British Columbia for many years prior to the date of this accident. The evidence will show that that is the section of the river that Ron Thompson had been over 200 times without incident. That is the same section that John McAlpine will tell you he took 12 people down in one raft an hour and a half before the raft in which this accident occurred departed."

Swindal would also have to dispel the notion that Jim Fasules was a city slicker who knew nothing about rivers.

"What did Jim Fasules know about whitewater rafting? I believe the evidence will show that he was a man very familiar with rivers and waterways. He was a fisherman. As a fisherman, there will be pictures in this case showing him standing in those waders. You move into fast waters when you fly-fish. The rocks are slippery. You have to be careful because if you fall in a hole that may or may not be seen, those waders will fill with water. So Jim was familiar with the power and attributes of water.

"Jim Fasules was invited as a last-minute fill-in by Al Wolfe because Needham's lawyer, Phil Reiss, couldn't make it. At the time, Gene Yovetich was fishing in Montana with Jim Fasules. Telephone calls were made, and on the telephone were Al Wolfe, Jim Fasules, and a third person, Mary Kahan, who will be here to testify as well. Mary was Al Wolfe's administrative assistant, executive secretary. She will tell you that during that telephone conversation—as will Al Wolfe—that Al said, 'Jim, would you like to go fishing and whitewater rafting with Gene Yovetich and some others in British Columbia? I can tell you that there will be great steelhead trout, and there will be 45 minutes of the wildest, woolliest whitewater that you have ever experienced or seen in your life.'

"The evidence will be that Jim Fasules accepted. He decided he wanted to go, and go he did. There was no pressure on Jim to go. He was eager. The men arrived at the airport in Vancouver. I think the restaurant was called The Boathouse. The men were coming from various parts of the country. They were gathering in the restaurant and having coffee, and they were talking. They were talking about the trip. They were excited. One of the gentlemen, Bob Goldstein, had fallen out of a boat on a prior trip, and they were giving him the needle. They were saying, 'Are we going to have to save you on this one, too?'

"They were talking about the Chilko River. The men who had been on the Chilko in 1985 were describing it—the big holes. 'You are going to get cold and wet.' There was an air of excitement, and Jim Fasules was there.

"When they went on the trip that Thursday and half of the group rafted, they came back around the campfire that night, and one of the topics of conversation was the excitement and the description of the Chilko River that they rafted that day. To those who had gone fishing the evidence will be, 'You should have gone with us. We had a ball. It's great. Big holes, excitement.'

"Now, they camped, and they camped in pairs or in groups. Earl Madsen shared a tent with Jim Fasules. Earl Madsen will tell you on the stand that Jim told him that he was looking forward to whitewater rafting on Saturday. When Saturday came and they were to embark, no one forced anybody into the raft to go rafting. If there was any concern at all, all they had to do was get in the van and drive to the Taseko junction to the take-out point. James Fasules and the other men chose to raft.

"I submit, ladies and gentlemen, that there will be no evidence in this case that Jim Fasules did not know what he was doing, that he was pressured to go rafting, that he was forced against his own judgment to raft.

"The only contrary evidence will come from Les Bechdel, who is being paid by the plaintiff to come in here and give you his opinion. Mr. Bechdel admitted in his deposition that James Fasules knew that if he got in a raft and went whitewater rafting, he could fall out and drown. Unfortunately, that's what happened. Les Bechdel had never in his life seen the Chilko River until July of 1989."

As he spoke, Swindal looked straight into the eyes of the jury members, and he exuded the sincerity of an advocate absolutely convinced that his client had done no wrong.

"You should listen to all the evidence, of course, but I ask that you listen to the evidence of the witnesses who were in Lava Canyon that August 1—to Earl Madsen, to John McAlpine, to Al Wolfe, to Ron Thompson, to Jack Collins. We will also offer the testimony of two expert witnesses from British Columbia—Jim Lavalley and Dan Culver. Jim Lavalley ran a rafting company through Lava Canyon. Dan Culver was the first person, to our knowledge, to have taken a kayak through Lava Canyon in 1972. None of these witnesses will find any wrongdoing. No one who was there on August 1, 1987, or who investigated it afterward placed any blame on Al Wolfe or Ron Thompson.

"Ladies and gentlemen, the evidence will show that this was simply and tragically an accident. At the time of the accident all the men were wearing approved life jackets. The raft was proper—it was a self-bailing, state-of-the-art raft, and it was loaded within manufacturer's recommended specifications. It had been customized by Ron Thompson with additional safety devices. The evidence will also show that proper safety instructions were given and that Ron Thompson was the most qualified and competent guide to run the Chilko River based on his experience.

"Now, after the accident, the British Columbia coroner investigated the accident. That document is in evidence, and you will see it through the course of the trial. The coroner's court found that Thompson was competent. The court found that the raft was loaded within limits. The court found that adequate safety instructions were given. The court found that the cause of the accident was a sudden unexpected rush of water which caught a competent guide off guard. Ladies and gentlemen, the evidence will show that it was an accident. The coroner's court placed no blame on Ron Thompson.

"I will not get a chance to speak to you again until the closing argument. At that time I will ask you to enter a verdict in this case in favor of the defendant and against the plaintiffs, not only because they will be unable to prove their case but because Al Wolfe did nothing wrong to cause the death of James Fasules.

"Thank you."

# Chapter Four

On the evening of Wednesday, July 29, 1987, the final group of 11 executives gathered near the Vancouver airport at a small restaurant and bar known as "The Boathouse." As would be expected, everyone there was excited about the whitewater rafting trip ahead of them, and the various conversations scattered among the small groups of men were lively and animated.

Those who had been on the Chilko River two years earlier were talking enthusiastically about the size of the holes in the river. They described the experience as "cold and wet," particularly the rapids known as White Mile. Someone mentioned that Goldstein had fallen out of the raft on one of their earlier rafting trips to Idaho, and the others gave him a good-natured ribbing about the incident.

While still in the bar, Art Wolfe asked Stu Sharpe, the young Needham executive, if he would circulate a release-and-assumption-of-the-risk form to everyone for their signatures. Each of the men hurriedly (and nonchalantly) signed the document and continued their drinking and socializing before their flights left.

The group of 11 men soon boarded two small Piper Chieftains to pierce the interior of British Columbia. As dusk was setting in, the planes flew over a dramatic panorama of dense forests and mountain peaks draped with snow. Their destination was the Chilko Lake Lodge, and an hour and a half later, they landed on a dirt airstrip carved out of the mountainside. They spent the night at a beautiful secluded lodge built in the 1940s, surrounded by rustic log cabins outfitted with all the modern conveniences.

On Thursday morning, the men were offered a choice between fishing or rafting as their activity for the day. Six of the men chose rafting, and they boarded a van and drove an hour farther into the wilderness. They were bound for the whitewater of Lava Canyon with a young guide named John McAlpine, who worked for the outfitter Ron Thompson. This group included the following:

Mike Miles
Dick O'Reilly
Stuart Sharpe
Art Wolfe
Gene Yovetich
Arthur Zeikel

The other men chose to go fishing instead:

Jack Collins
Jim Fasules
Bob Goldstein
Earl Madsen
Joe Morrison

As it turned out, five of the men on the trip—Jim Fasules, Bob Goldstein, Dick O'Reilly, Stuart Sharpe, and Gene Yovetich—would have only another 48 hours to live.

After a day of rafting and fishing, the group reconvened and camped about a mile from the Chilko Lake Lodge. Those who had gone rafting told the others that it was a day of grand excitement, and they described in detail the large reversals in the river's currents as they came crashing through the maelstrom.

When the men arose on Friday morning, it was cold and damp, having rained heavily all night, causing the river to rise several feet, the second-highest level it had been in the past five years. The weather had declined so much that several of the men suggested that they return to the lodge, and a few even considered going home. But the group persisted, and they traveled farther downstream on the placid river, where they camped once again.

For dinner that night, the outfitter served a delicious meal of cooked Cornish game hen and wild rice, along with carrots, onions, and zucchini grilled over an open fire. The dessert was a delicious strawberry shortcake baked in a Dutch oven set over the coals. Everyone was in a jovial mood, and they were enjoying the escape from the bustle of the city and the heavy responsibilities of their lucrative positions.

Standing around the campfire, these well-heeled men drank beer and wine, and the conversation was filled with tall tales of fishing journeys from around the world. Dick O'Reilly told his usual corny jokes. There was a serious discussion of the Iran-Contra affair, which dominated the news of the day. Naturally, there was business banter about the world of advertising and marketing. And Bob Goldstein engaged in a friendly but intense argument about politics with a young woman who had just graduated from college and who had been hired to drive one of the outfitter's vans.

That night, Earl Madsen shared a tent with Jim Fasules, who mentioned how much he was looking forward to whitewater rafting on Saturday, even though he had never been before. The clouds over the river canyon slowly cleared, and the Milky Way appeared.

Saturday promised to be a marvelous day. Most of those in the camp were up early, and by 6:00 a.m., the men were ready for a hearty breakfast of eggs Benedict and sausage. A van arrived, and all of their luggage and personal gear was packed inside. The van drove away, leaving Thompson and the 11 men alone at the campsite. The waters of the Chilko, pale green with glacial silt, swept swiftly by.

Soon, another van pulled up with the guide John McAlpine behind the wheel, along with a number of strangers inside. Attached to the van was a trailer with a raft, and it soon drove away. Several of the members of the Needham group appeared confused. Bob Goldstein, who was a veteran of numerous raft trips, approached Art Wolfe and said, "I thought there were going to be two rafts." Wolfe replied, "So did I. But what the hell, let's have fun anyway."

Thompson seemed to take a long time arranging the scattered and disorganized mounds of equipment—raft, rowing frame, bow and stern lines, life jackets, throw ropes, air pump, repair materials, first aid kit, and lunch supplies. The executives—who were used to the fast pace of the corporate world—stood waiting, impatiently. Eventually, Thompson told everyone to put on their life jackets, and he checked each one of them to make sure that they fit snugly.

At long last, the group boarded a single 18-foot-long raft: a brand-new boat manufactured with the latest high-tech materials and a state-of-the-art self-bailing floor. Thompson told the men where to sit, and he instructed them to tightly hold on to the metal rowing frame while they were in the rapids. Thompson pushed the large raft from shore, clambered aboard, and took his place in the middle of the raft, where he grabbed the 11-foot-long ash oars and rowed the boat into the glistening current.

For about 90 minutes, the river was swift but without any hazards. Several of the men asked about maneuvering the boat, and Thompson showed several of them how to row and turn the boat. When they arrived at Bidwell Rapids, Thompson took over the oars again. The rapids were mild and, in the minds of some, a little anticlimactic. The group then stopped briefly to have a light lunch of cheese and crackers. The raft was slightly soft, having lost some air, and Thompson inflated it with a small hand pump.

The men who were sitting in the back of the raft complained that they were not getting enough whitewater thrills, and they said that they would change places with those in the front. The lone exception was Al Wolfe, an experienced rafter who remained in the bow in order to get as much action as possible.

After lunch, the group pushed off from shore, and the roar of rapids grew louder and louder as they moved downstream. They soon entered the much-anticipated rapids known as White Kilometer. The men enjoyed the ride through the boisterous rapids, and everyone on board was in high spirits. Next up was White Mile, the stretch of cataracts with the most foreboding reputation of all.

When the raft was about 200 yards into the maw of White Mile, the rafters noticed a large flat rock to the left that extended about five feet above the surface of the water. Several of the men noticed that Thompson was having trouble rowing the heavy boat, which was headed straight toward the rock. The raft then unexpectedly punched through the pillow of water forming around the rock.

In reaction, Thompson quickly jumped from the center of the boat, and with one knee on the tube, he leaned forward and tried to push the raft away from the large boulder.

About the time the raft hit the rock, Thompson yelled to the others, "High side!" so that they could all move to that side of the raft to prevent it from moving up on its side. But it was too late. In a matter of seconds, the raft was on its side, perpendicular to the river, pouring its passengers into the churning waves of the Chilko. Surprisingly enough, the raft did not flip. Everyone but Jack Collins fell into the cold river, where they were forcibly plunged beneath the water.

Thompson was able to quickly escape the raging river. He saw Jim Fasules within arm's distance, grabbed him, and pulled him to shore. Thompson asked if he was alright, and Fasules nodded that he was. Thompson ran quickly toward the road to get help.

The scene in the river was quickly becoming chaotic. The swift river scattered the men along the length and breadth of the river.

Joe Morrison surfaced after he hit the bottom of the river and was able to swim toward the shore. He grabbed a tree branch and was holding on as tight as he could while the current pulled and stretched him out horizontally. He was finally able to pull himself onto the bank, and from the river, he heard a voice moaning with pain. It was Morrison's mentor, Richard O'Reilly, who floated downstream and out of sight.

Across the river, Morrison could see Arthur Zeikel on the opposite shore. Morrison was soon joined on the bank by Mike Miles, who clawed his way out of the river. Morrison and Miles tried to scale the steep canyon wall, but they kept sliding down the unstable scree.

Morrison and Miles peered downstream, and they could see Jack Collins in the raft flailing away at the oars, trying to control the boat. Collins, who was in the center of the disaster, looked over and watched Robert Goldstein—who was clearly dead—float slowly and quietly by the raft. Then suddenly, Jim Fasules appeared out of nowhere next to the boat, unable to move. Collins tried desperately to pull Jim into the raft by grabbing his life jacket, but the jacket was too loose, and the attempt was useless.

Unbeknownst to Collins, Earl Madsen was all the while clinging to the bottom of the raft. When Collins realized Madsen's predicament, he tried to pull Madsen in, but Madsen was a large man, and the churning rapids washed him downriver. Collins finally gained control of the raft, and Madsen was able to grasp a bush alongside the shore to stop his progress downstream. Collins and Madsen eventually stumbled onto land, and Madsen was clearly suffering from a dangerous condition of hypothermia. Collins tore off Madsen's clothes—as well as his own—to restore the temperature of Madsen's body core, and he bravely saved his friend's life. When the two regained their composure, they began their walk to the road and were spotted by a helicopter and flown to civilization.

Meanwhile, stranded on the banks, Morrison and Miles looked upstream to see that Ron Thompson had returned with another raft. Thompson was uncharacteristically shaken, realizing that this was no longer a rescue mission but a recovery for bodies. Morrison and Miles boarded the raft with Thompson, and Thompson rowed across the river to pick up Zeikel.

A few miles downstream, Thompson and the three others in the raft came across Wolfe, who was on the shore. Wolfe was pale white and shook uncontrollably from hypothermia. He had been in the water for 45 minutes as he grabbed whatever vegetation he could find along the canyon walls to try to keep from being flushed farther down the canyon.

Seven of the men were now accounted for. As the day wore on, the bodies of five others were slowly recovered by boat or helicopter along the river corridor: first, James Fasules; then Bob Goldstein; next, Dick O'Reilly, then Gene Yovetich; and, finally, Stu Sharpe.

Most of the victims were wearing jeans or shorts and running shoes and maybe a sweater or light jacket. A few of them had life jackets that for some reason had come undone. Some of the men sustained severe cuts and bruises to their faces and upper bodies. The hospital at the small village of Alexis Creek was set up as a makeshift morgue, and Al Wolfe and Gene Madsen were asked to confirm the identities of the bodies, some of which were difficult to recognize due to the battering they had received.

Among this desperately tragic scene, Al Wolfe now had the unenviable task of calling the families of the deceased to tell them what had happened to their loved ones.

# Chapter Five

Faced with the sudden loss of her husband of 39 years, Lenore Fasules was convinced that Jim had died because of the negligence of others. She felt that she had no other choice than to sue Jim's former employer, DDB Needham, for his death, and she did so in the fall of 1989 in a federal district court in Chicago, where the corporate headquarters of DDB Needham was located.

At the time of the trial, it had been a little more than two years since Jim Fasules had drowned in the foam of the Chilko River. Like all lawsuits in which liability is not clear-cut, the trial promised to be a duel to the end, and both Lenore Fasules and DDB Needham hired extremely competent Chicago counsel. In the end, the trial was as contentious and hard fought as expected. The testimony during the dramatic two-week trial was high drama. The chilling stories of the men who survived the ordeal and the terse opinions of the experts who evaluated what went wrong on were riveting—and sometimes dramatically inconsistent.

For example, Earl Madsen described the harrowing events that day:

Q. Do you recall what happened then? Which way did the raft go?
A. The raft hit absolutely in the center and just stopped on the rock.
Q. Dead in the water?
A. Dead in the water. Ron had jumped down on the front edge of the raft, as he saw we were coming into the rock, to push off with his hands. I was totally unconcerned. I had been in many raft situations where we have pushed off rocks and snags. So he was trying to push off the rock with his knee. He was down on one knee on the edge of the front edge of the raft.

Q. About where you were sitting? Do you want to come and show the jury? He came off the ice chest?

A. Right. And moved down to this side [indicating], on the side of the rubber raft. As I recall, he had one foot on the floor of the raft and his knee on the side, and he pushed on the raft. He turned around and he said, "Everybody get to the rock side," and that was the first time I knew we were in trouble.

Q. The next thing you recall, where were you?

A. I was at the bottom of the river. I had no recollection of the raft being anything but perfectly horizontal and stable. I had no sense of the raft tipping or moving, but I just went straight down, and I remember hitting the bottom of the river just like this on my back [indicating].

Q. Like a snap of the fingers and you were on the bottom of ——?

A. Absolutely. I had no idea we were going to have a problem.

Another member of the group, Jack Collins—who was the only one to remain in the raft after the collision—testified about seeing several of those who had drowned:

Q. One of the first persons that you saw in the water was Bob Goldstein, wasn't he, sir?

A. Yes, sir.

Q. I mean, the bodies were kind of all together, but you saw Bob Goldstein in the water?

A. Yes, sir, that's correct.

Q. Isn't it a fact that he was either dead or semiconscious when you first saw him there in the water?

A. That's the way he looked to me, yes, sir.

Q. He had lost his glasses. Is that right?

A. Yes, sir.

Q. His face at that time had an expression of both strain and surprise?

A. Yes, sir.

Q. His eyes were open, but unlike the eyes of some of the others in the water, they didn't seem to be moving or focused—isn't that right?

A. That's correct, sir.

Collins also saw Jim Fasules in the water struggling to stay alive as he floated by the raft:

Q. Sometime shortly after the 11 men fell overboard, you realized that Jim Fasules was next to the raft and that you could reach him, didn't you, sir?
A. Yes, sir.
Q. He was conscious, was he not?
A. Yes, sir.
Q. And his eyes and his lips—his lips were moving?
A. I believe so, yes, sir. His eyes were moving certainly.
Q. And his eyes were saying to you "please help me"?
A. That is the way I interpreted it, yes, sir.
Q. But he didn't say anything?
A. No, sir.
Q. He couldn't raise up his arms because the life jacket was up pretty high on him?
A. I don't know, but his arms were not up. His arms were underwater.
Q. And you grasped his jacket, didn't you, sir?
A. Yes, sir.
Q. You saw that you were pulling it up higher?
A. Yes, sir. It already appeared to be too high on his body. And when I pulled on it, it moved further up his body.
Q. You realized that you couldn't help him, so you let him go?
A. Yes, sir.

The factual issues presented in the courthouse during the two-week-long trial were numerous and provocative:

• Who was responsible for making the decision to take only one raft—the outfitter Ron Thompson or the organizer Al Wolfe on behalf of DDB Needham?
• Did anyone tell Jim Fasules about the size and severity of the rapids in Lava Canyon?
• Did Fasules have sufficient knowledge of the river hazards to consent to this risky endeavor?
• Were the life jackets adequate for the intensity of the river?

- What safety instructions were provided by the outfitter to those who might fall out of the raft?
- Would a rescue kayaker or second raft have saved these men's lives?

The witnesses in the courtroom gave inconsistent versions of the events that day. Jack Collins was adamant that Ron Thompson provided *no* safety instructions at to the group, Earl Madsen said that Thompson provided *some* instructions, and Al Wolfe was unequivocal that Thompson discussed *all* the necessary safety procedures, which he specified in detail.

The legal issues in the trial were difficult to resolve:

- Was Thompson negligent in using only one raft, which was arguably overloaded?
- Was Thompson negligent in the breadth and scope of his safety instructions?
- Were the life jackets sufficiently tightened to keep them from slipping off the men's bodies?
- Was Thompson at fault in failing to supply wetsuits and helmets?
- Was Thompson careless by not providing more throw ropes as well as instructions on how to use them?
- Was the organizer of the trip, DDB Needham, ultimately responsible for any negligence of the rafting outfitter?
- What was the effect of the release-and-assumption-of-the-risk form that the passengers signed before the trip relieving the outfitter of any responsibility?

There were also subtle issues of peer pressure among those on the trip:

- Were the junior account executives from Needham coerced—even subtly—into joining the trip in order to advance their careers?
- Did some of those lost their lives proceed downriver in order to avoid being labeled as cowards?

And finally, there was the shocking testimony of the outfitter Ron Thompson late in the trial that he had in fact plucked Jim Fasules out of the river and swam him to shore before he left the river to get help.

The inevitable question arose: how did Jim Fasules then get *back* into the river—where he was later seen by Jack Collins floating beside the raft with his eyes darting and his lips trembling with fear?

In spite of the fact that Jim Fasules had executed a release-and-assumption-of-the-risk form, the jury ultimately decided that he was 45 percent responsible for his own death and that Needham was 55 percent responsible. The jury awarded the Fasules family $1.1 million in damages.

Three decades later, the answers to the many of the questions raised in the trial are still unresolved. What exactly happened that horrendous day at White Mile—and how the jury should have ruled in resolving the unspeakable tragedy in this most strangely alluring of outdoor pursuits—is still largely a mystery.

# Chapter Six

To prosecute her case against Needham in federal court, Lenore Fasules hired an attorney named Brian Crowe, a senior partner, and Phillip Goldberg, his junior associate, from the well-respected Chicago law firm of Coffield, Ungaretti, Harris & Slavin.

To defend itself in the litigation, DDB Needham brought in William Swindal, the senior partner, and Debra Davy, the junior associate, from the prestigious firm of Hinshaw, Culbertson, Moelmann, Hoban & Fuller firm, also of Chicago.

These were very experienced courtroom litigators eager to assert the sharply opposing positions of their clients, and they worked prodigiously to provide the best legal representation possible.

This was clearly not your typical wrongful death case. The most likely defendant would have been Ron Thompson, the owner of the small rafting and fishing company located in the hamlet of Alexis Creek, British Columbia. Thomson was in charge of *all* the logistics, equipment, and guiding services for the Chilko trip, and it was he who was rowing the raft through the rapids of White Mile in which the five men drowned. But rather than sue Thompson, the counsel for Lenore Fasules decided—not unexpectedly—to pursue the deep pockets of DDB Needham, the multinational corporation that sponsored and paid for the trip as part of its client development program.

The plaintiff's lawyers no doubt considered several factors before filing suit. The cost and inconvenience of trying the case in British Columbia, where the accident occurred and the outfitter was based, were unappealing. The law of Canada governing compensation for personal injury victims was less generous. There was the concern that the locals, wise in the ways of the outdoors, might not have much sympathy for the rich city slickers who had assumed the risks of running a dangerous whitewater river. Besides, the outfitter had neither the assets nor even an insurance liability policy on which to execute a judgment.

The plaintiff in every lawsuit typically encounters at least one unique dilemma. In this case, Lenore Fasules faced the challenge of turning Art Wolfe—the intelligent, reliable, articulate, and affable individual that he was—into a savvy, money-hungry manipulator. Lenore would have to do this in order to arouse sympathy for her husband and to overcome the presumption that the outfitter of the trip—not the sponsor of the trip—should be liable for any negligence.

In his opening statement, Brian Crowe, Lenore's first-rate litigator, wasted no time in this characterization: "Art Wolfe developed client relationships and a business promotion through power and what we now call or what the advertising company calls *macho*. He was indeed a macho man, and it goes way back."

To transfer liability for Jim's death from Thompson to DDB Needham, Lenore would have to prove that Al Wolfe—not Ron Thompson—was the *actual* cause of Jim Fasules's death. This would be done, first, by showing that Wolfe directed Thompson to take only one raft and thus imperil the life of her husband and, second, by showing that Wolfe failed to warn Jim Fasules of the dangerous situation he was getting himself into and thus could not fully consent to the venture and thereby release any claims against the outfitter for negligence.

Brian Crowe made these poignant points in his opening statement: "Al Wolfe knew the dangers of the Chilko River, and what is worse, he knew the precautions that had to be taken—precautions like two rafts and precautions like never having more than six to eight people in a raft. He knew the dangers. He knew the precautions."

The other problem Lenore faced was the witnesses who were actually at the scene of the accident. All were friends and professional colleagues of Art Wolfe, who became for all practical purposes the defendant. And friends don't typically implicate their friends in lawsuits and thus expose them to large monetary judgments.

Surprising enough, Lenore found a sympathetic fact witness in Jack Collins, the president and chief executive officer of The Clorox Company, who had been a longtime business colleague of Wolfe. Collins had worked at Procter & Gamble when Needham was handling the P&G account under Wolfe's watchful eye. Collins considered Wolfe a close personal friend, and he said so at trial. The two men had been on a number of whitewater rafting trips together.

Collins's best friend was Bob Goldstein, vice president of marketing for Procter & Gamble, who drowned on the Chilko and whose widow had also sued Needham for the death of her husband. It is reasonable to assume that Collins was trying to assist the widows of Goldstein and Fasules in their efforts to recover compensation for the death of their husbands. Jack Collins knew that his friend and colleague Al Wolfe would never have to pay the judgment. Needham—or its insurer—would have to do that.

Collins, as might be expected of an individual in his position, exuded an air of dignity and truthfulness when he stepped inside the courtroom. In his testimony, Collins brought to the table some extremely damaging testimony about the way the raft trip was handled, particularly what he claimed was a grossly negligent act by Thompson—the lack of *any* whitewater safety instructions.

Collins also possessed a unique—and very advantageous—vantage point on the river. He was the only person, including guide Ron Thompson, who did *not* fall out of the raft. He had a remarkable view with which to see all that was going on as the raft neared the boulder and collided and everyone spilled into the river. As he watched the disaster unfurl, Collins tried to rescue several of those who floated by, including Jim Fasules. In somber and measured tones, Collins gave the jury his account of the accident. It was the drama that all of them been anticipating.

Collins first described what happened to Goldstein, who appeared to be dead as he floated stiff and glassy-eyed down the river. The description was chilling, and the drop of a pin could be heard in the courtroom. Lenore's attorney, the venerable Brian Crowe, had Collins begin his story in the moments immediately before the collision, when Thompson gave the "high side" command for everyone to quickly shift to the downstream side of the raft in order to keep it from wrapping around the boulder and filling with water. The jury was left with the distinct impression that Thompson's instructions were too little, too late.

Crowe leaned into the drama of the moment as he interrogated Collins. "But, as you sit here today, you don't recall when Thompson yelled 'high side'?"

"No, sir. It could have been after impact. It could have been just before. It could have been at the moment of impact. It all happened so quickly."

Crowe continued. "You were the only one to remain in the raft, weren't you? The other 11 men were all thrown into the Chilko River in the White Mile?"

"Ten of the other 11 men I know were thrown into the river. I heard subsequently that Mr. Thompson jumped onto the rock and was never actually in the water, but all were thrown out of the raft."

"You were the only one that remained there—is that correct?"

"Yes, sir."

Collins then spoke hauntingly of Bob Goldstein. Crowe, the skilled trial attorney that he was, set up the morbid scene of Goldstein floating quietly and lifelessly downstream with his eyes glazed over and a confused expression on his face. "One of the first persons that you saw in the water was Bob Goldstein, wasn't he, sir?"

"Yes, sir."

"I mean, the bodies were kind of all together, but you saw Bob Goldstein in the water?"

"Yes, sir, that's correct."

"Isn't it a fact that he was either dead or semiconscious when you first saw him there in the water?"

"That's the way he looked to me, yes, sir."

"He had lost his glasses. Is that right?" asked Crowe.

"Yes, sir."

"His face at that time had an expression of both strain and surprise?"

"Yes, sir."

"His eyes were open, but unlike the eyes of some of the others in the water, they didn't seem to be moving or focused—isn't that right?"

"That's correct, sir."

Make no mistake about it: Crowe's interrogation of Collins was a blatant example of leading a witness on direct examination, which is of course forbidden by the court's procedural rules. But counsel for Needham never once objected, presumably because their protestations would have brought even greater attention to the damaging testimony.

Crowe asked Collins about Jim Fasules. Collins spoke emotionally of this quiet, timid man who floated close to the raft, pleading for help with his darting eyes and trembling lips. Collins said that he reached over the raft to grab Jim's life jacket, but he quickly realized that it was so loose-fitting that it would be pulled off. Collins simply had to let him go, and Jim floated silently downstream.

Crowe poignantly inquired of Collins, "Sometime shortly after the 11 men fell overboard, you realized that Jim Fasules was next to the raft and that you could reach him, didn't you, sir?"

"Yes, sir."

"He was conscious, was he not?" asked Crowe.

"Yes, sir."

"And his eyes and his lips—his lips were moving?"

"I believe so, yes, sir. His eyes were moving certainly."

"And his eyes were saying to you 'please help me'?"

"That is the way I interpreted it, yes, sir," answered Collins.

"But he didn't say anything?"

"No, sir."

"He couldn't raise up his arms because the life jacket was up pretty high on him?"

"I don't know whether he couldn't, but his arms were not up. His arms were underwater."

"And you grasped his jacket, didn't you, sir?" asked Crowe.

"Yes, sir."

"You saw that all you were doing was pulling it up higher?"

"Yes, sir. It already appeared to be too high on his body. And when I pulled on it—I moved it further up his body."

"You realized that you couldn't help him, so you let him go?"

"Yes, sir."

Crowe then asked Collins to talk about the fate of the others. Collins described three individuals—Michael Miles, Joe Morrison, and Art Zeikel—as they desperately struggled to reach a safe place in the angry river.

Crowe pressed forward, "And you recall seeing a guy in a red jacket grab a hold of a bush on the right of the river, isn't that right?"

"Yes, sir. That was somewhat later, I believe."

"You are thinking to yourself, 'How is he ever going to hang on because that current was pulling his body out horizontally.'"

"More than that, I thought he was probably not going to hang on."

"That was Joe Morrison, wasn't it?" asked Crowe.

"I figured out later that it was."

"Mike Miles and Art Zeikel got out of the water pretty quickly, didn't they?"

"Zeikel got out of the water very quickly. Mike Miles got out essentially in the same place that Joe Morrison did because they were together."

"Ron Thompson, of course, he got out pretty quickly, too?"

"Yes, sir."

Crowe asked Collins about the fate of the others who went into the water, and the answer was unsettling. "So, the guys that got out right away did okay and they survived?"

"Yes, that's correct."

"You survived because you were in the raft?"

"That's correct," said Collins.

"Mr. Madsen was able to hang onto the raft until you finally were able to tie it to a tree? We'll talk about that in a minute."

"Essentially, yes, sir."

"But of the people that went down the river, other than Al Wolfe, everyone died—isn't that right?"

"Yes, sir, that's correct."

Collins described the chaotic scene of the raft being tossed around in the tumultuous river after the accident. The jury was riveted on the scene being unfurled before them.

Crowe asked the gripping question, "Can you describe to us the action of the raft with you in it as it was going through these rapids immediately before and after you had to let go of Mr. Fasules?"

"Yes" replied Collins. "The raft was spinning around, and I was unable to control it. I had the oars. I lost one of the oars at one point. I was unable to control the raft in terms of direction. I later found out it was because Mr. Madsen was holding onto the side and acting like a kind of anchor. But the raft was basically spinning out of control through the rapids."

"Do you recall the sound of that river as it was tearing through that canyon?"

"Yes, sir."

"Would you describe it for us, sir?"

"It was like a locomotive in a tunnel, a roaring sound."

Collins then moved to a discussion of Earl Madsen, Wolfe's lawyer friend from Colorado, who was somehow able to latch onto the raft while Collins struggled to control the raft with the oars. Crowe asked Collins what exactly happened. "Now, all of a sudden—it kind of surprised you—Earl Madsen grabbed a hold of that raft, didn't he?"

"Yes. I am not clear when Earl Madsen first grabbed hold of the raft. It may have been—he says he came up under the raft, and when he came out from under it, he was able to grab a hold of it. I don't know when I first became aware of him in relation to seeing Mr. Fasules or Mr. Goldstein or Mr. Wolfe or any of the others."

"As Madsen held onto the raft, he kind of acted like a sea anchor, didn't he?"

"Yes, sir. He was slowing the raft down and making it difficult or impossible for me to control the direction."

Crowe asked Collins if he had stopped rowing in order to try and pull Madsen inside the boat. "He at one point shouted for you to pull him in the raft and help him out, isn't that right?"

"Yes, sir."

"What did you try to do?"

"I put the oars inside the raft, and I reached over the side of the raft, and I grasped his right wrist with my hand. He grasped my wrist with his hand, and I tried to lift him on board."

"Were you able to do that?"

"No, sir, not at all."

"Could you tell us why?"

"Yes, sir. He is a big man, and I don't have a great deal of upper body strength. Also, the raft is so big around, and I was standing in the bottom leaning over trying to pull him on board, and I just didn't have the ability to do it."

Madsen then disappeared into the maw of the churning rapids. Crowe asked, "Can you tell us a little more about that as Madsen was trying to get in the raft? What happened then? What happened next?"

"Well, I was having a crisis of conscience because I realized that I had made a mistake in grabbing hold of him because I now had absolutely no control over the raft or of him, and I was concerned about letting go of him. I realized I had made a mistake, but I didn't quite know what to do. Then we went into a very heavy rapid, and it was solved for me because I lost contact with him, and that was it, sir."

In the meantime, Collins said that he watched a limp life jacket float slowly down the river. The body was all but underwater, and it turned out to be Dick O'Reilly. Crowe resumed his questioning. "At about this time did you see a life jacket floating in the water?"

"Yes, sir. I saw a life jacket floating in the water, and I can't place in my mind whether it was before or after this episode with Mr. Madsen, but in the course all events are all mixed up in my mind, but at some point yes, sir, I did see a life jacket in the water."

"And there was a body in that life jacket?"

"Yes," replied Collins.

"And it was fully underwater?"

"The body was fully underwater and the life jacket was on the surface."

Crowe continued. "And you thought at one time that it was Stu Sharpe, but it actually you think that is Dick O'Reilly, don't you, sir?"

"Yes, sir. I think I originally thought it was Dick O'Reilly, but then I became convinced wrongly that it was Stu Sharpe, and now I am convinced because I remember the clothing that it was Dick O'Reilly."

The jury was clearly anxious to hear more. With measured cadence, Collins spoke of Madsen's rescue. Crowe had a general request: "Can you tell us how you eventually saved yourself and Mr. Madsen—how you got this raft to shore? What happened?"

"Well, I kept pulling on the oars, and I guess I was fortunate [to get] into an eddy that carried us to the east side of the river, and I realized that Earl—who happened to be on that side of the raft—at that point could grab a hold of some branches, and he didn't see them. So I shouted to him, 'Turn round and grab the branches,' and he did. As soon as he let go, I found I could indeed maneuver the raft. So I rowed it to shore."

"Okay. And then when you finally got to the shore, what happened then? You got out of the raft?" asked Crowe.

"I got out of the raft and I tied it to a tree, and I sat next to the raft. I was shaking and a little disoriented, I guess, and then I heard Earl calling to me, and I realized he was just little bit away."

"Did he come to you?"

"No, he called me to come to him because he was cold and undergo-ing hypothermia," responded Collins.

"He was suffering hypothermia? How could you tell?"

"Just because I know what it is and he was shivering uncontrollably and he was lucid but semi-coherent and just all of the symptoms that I have become generally aware of."

"And what did you do to help him with that condition?"

"Well, I tried to impart some body heat, but it initially didn't work because I still had my life jacket on, and he had his life jacket on. So I took off my life jacket and took off his life jacket and took off my shirt and took off his shirt and cut away his windbreaker, and then I embraced him on shore with—you know—naked torsos. And after just a few minutes, he started to get warm, and I started to get cold. So it had worked."

The testimony revealed that at about 5:00, Collins and Madsen, cold and wet, started their hike out of the canyon. It was getting dark, and they were wearing only shorts and tennis shoes. They reached a meadow when they spotted a helicopter that landed and picked them up.

Collins testified about the difficult task of identifying his colleagues at the end of the day after their bodies had been pulled from the river. Some of the corpses were very difficult to recognize. Crowe asked the grisly question. "You eventually identified the bodies, sir, did you?"

"Yes, I did."

"You identified Jim Fasules and Bob Goldstein straightforward, didn't you?"

"No problem, yes, sir."

"But the third body was a little more difficult for you to identify. And that is because the face was smashed and badly beaten?"

"In part. The other part was that I had been told that Stu Sharpe's body had been found and that both Dick O'Reilly and Gene Yovetich's bodies had not yet been found. I was tired and by the process of elimina-tion—since people had told me that Stu Sharpe's body had been found and there were three bodies—I was able to positively identify two of them. I made the logical but totally wrong assumption that this was Stu Sharpe."

"And it was really O'Reilly?" asked Crowe.

"It was really O'Reilly."

"But in large part, your mistake was caused by the fact that the face was badly smashed and beaten?"

"Yes, sir."

Crowe resumed. "Sir, is it true that of the three friends that you identified—Jim Fasules, Bob Goldstein, and Dick O'Reilly—that Bob was the only one who had a peaceful expression on his face?"

"Yes, sir."

"Sir, is it a fact that you—that you didn't realize the anger of the Chilko River until this raft tipped over?"

"That is correct."

Crowe proceeded to drill into the most incriminating piece of testimony—the lack of rescue instructions from Thompson.

"Mr. Collins, there were no instructions given to you by Thompson about how to pull someone in the raft if they fell in?"

"No, sir."

"And there was no instructions to you about how to throw a rope to somebody, either, by Thompson?"

"No, sir."

Collins testified that two rafts were present on the river that fateful day, but the other group of rafters—the non-Needham people—used one of them. The van with the other raft drove to a point downriver with Ron's assistant, John McAlpine, as the guide. It was not revealed how many people were in the other group. Was it three, four, 10? Collins did not say.

The other question that was not directly asked—and the most pressing one—was whether the division among the two rafting groups was the result of Wolfe's insistence that only Needham people be allowed in their group—which then forced the 11 men into a single boat with Thompson as guide.

In his opening statement, Crowe had predicted, "I believe the evidence is going to show that it was Thompson's non–decision-making personality in response to Wolfe's aggressive personality in demanding privacy of his group that led to Jim Fasules's death."

Crowe pressed the issue with Collins. "At this point. you all believed that you were going to float down the rapids in two rafts, didn't you, sir?"

"Yes, sir, we did. May I correct myself, sir?"

"Yes, sir."

"I believed it. Al Wolfe believed it. I think most of the other people believed there were going to be two rafts, but I don't know that for sure. I know that I believed it."

Collins was asked whether there was any concern about the safety of a single-boat trip and whether masculine pride had prevented anyone from protesting. "Is it true, sir, that everybody was concerned about it?"

"I can't answer that, sir. I was concerned about crowding. Wolfe agreed with me it was going to be too crowded, but I can't speak for the others. I don't know."

"Is it true that no one spoke up because, as you sit here today, you think that you all were under the spell of machismo?"

"Those are words that I used, but it was in the context of somebody hypothecating that Mr. Goldstein had a safety concern—which I don't know that he did—and it came up primarily in the coroner's interview. I was asked whether anybody had safety concerns, and I said I didn't really know. I didn't hear any expressed. Then I volunteered the statement that perhaps if they did, they didn't say anything because we were under the spell of machismo."

"In fact, you said that nobody wanted to play the wimp?"

"Yes, sir. I used those words."

Collins recalled the other commercial raft trips that he had taken. None of those trips involved only a single raft, and there were usually three or four rafts with no more than five or six people in each. Collins firmly believed that the weight of so many men caused the raft on the Chilko to become sluggish and more difficult to control.

Crowe proceeded to do the math for the jury. "Let's talk the weight for a moment. At that time, you weighed about 200 pounds. Did you not?"

"Yes, sir."

"And you were a little less than the average weight of the guys in that raft?"

"That would be my guess, yes, sir. There was one who was a little lighter than you, but the others weighed 225 pounds or more—didn't they, sir?"

"Yes, sir."

"And isn't it a fact—tell me if these were your words—'We had a hell of a lot of weight in the raft just of flesh and bone'?"

"Yes, sir, those are my words."

With the somber testimony of Jack Collins behind them, Needham's counsel, Debra Davy, had little material to cross-examine with except to point out that Jim Fasules had voluntarily engaged in an activity that was known at times to be dangerous. Collins admitted that the risks of whitewater boating are open and obvious and that even Al Wolfe, the experienced rafter he was, and Thompson, the professional guide, would *not* have gone down the river if they had thought it was unreasonably dangerous.

It appeared, then, that Jim Fasules had voluntarily committed to the venture—but did he really know what he was getting himself into?

Davy developed the theme as best she could. "Did Jim Fasules act in any way or say anything that caused you to believe that he did not want to raft on Saturday—a reluctance or anything like that?"

"No, he did not."

"Did you see anything in Jim Fasules's behavior or Al Wolfe's behavior that would demonstrate to you that Al Wolfe was controlling or directing Jim Fasules's behavior?"

"No, ma'am.

"Now, prior to this trip, I think you said you didn't fully appreciate the dangers of whitewater rafting this particular river?"

"That's correct," replied Collins.

"But did you know there was some risk?"

"Yes, clearly."

"Well, how is that?" asked Davy.

"Well, part of the adventure of whitewater rafting is that there is some risk or at least perceived risk involved. It's not in the magnitude of skydiving or mountain claiming, but it's certainly more than going to a baseball game or a golf outing."

Apparently, no one on the journey down the Chilko that day thought the endeavor was "unreasonably" dangerous. Davy continued with the line of questioning. "Do you have any reason to believe that Ron Thompson or Al Wolfe knew how dangerous it was and you didn't?"

"No, ma'am. I don't think that Ron Thompson or Al Wolfe thought it was dangerous or particularly dangerous, or they wouldn't have gone. Their lives were on the line, too, obviously."

Ron Thompson, who had taken over 200 trips down the Chilko without incident, had a stellar reputation in the professional rafting community, and no concerns were ever expressed by those on the river that day. Davy was careful to emphasize the point.

"Did you or anyone else tell Ron Thompson, 'This is unsafe. I don't want to do it'?"

"I did not speak to Ron Thompson about it. I spoke only to Al Wolfe, and I did not hear anyone else speak to Ron Thompson about it."

"And when you spoke to Al Wolfe, did you tell him you had feared for your safety?"

"No, I did not."

"If you had feared for your safety, would you have gotten on the raft?"

"No, I would not."

Davy delved further into the liability aspect of the case. She asked Collins if Al Wolfe directed Ron Thompson to use only one raft. Collins refused to implicate his friend Wolfe.

"Now, I want to talk about Saturday morning, again. I want to talk about the decision to go in one raft. Was it Al Wolfe who decided and directed the use of one raft rather than two?" asked Davy.

"No, ma'am. As I have testified before, I think I initiated the conversation by saying, 'Al, I thought we were going to have two rafts for this,' and he said something like, 'I thought so, too. But what the hell, there is only one. Let's just enjoy it and have fun.'"

"So Al Wolfe had expected there to be two rafts? Did Al Wolfe demand of Ron Thompson that all of you folks be put into one raft when you could have had two?"

"No, never."

"Did Ron Thompson at any time protest and say, 'All of you 11 men in one raft? No, not good'? Did that happen at all?"

"No. Never," replied Collins.

Davy then asked Collins if Wolfe had ever coerced Thompson to isolate the Needham group.

"Did Al Wolfe in any way direct Ron Thompson to have the other raft sent down the river ahead so it could be away from you men?"

Collins replied, "No, I don't believe Al was even a party to that decision. As I have testified, when the other raft arrived, we thought it was going to be our raft. But, instead, it was with a van full of people. They stopped and visited with Thompson for a few moments—I forget what they talked about—and then they drove away. Al was as surprised as the rest of us when it happened."

"Have you learned how many men were in that raft?"

"No, ma'am."

Davy continued. "Now, there has been some mention in this court-room about Al exerting pressure on Ron Thompson to keep the group exclusive."

"Do you know anything about that?"

"I did not hear Al make any such statements to Ron Thompson. I know that that was Al's desire. I don't care for the word 'exclusive' but prefer 'keep us an independent group.' I know it was because of a relatively unpleasant experience that we had on the Selway River in an earlier trip."

"What was it?"

"The guide in that case—a gentleman named Steve Curry—had put together a rafting group for us of perhaps 10 or 12 people in two or three rafts, and then he had added another raft with three or four additional people who we did not know and who were just the kind of people that we didn't care to associate with. One was a lady of rather loose morals, and two of them were using drugs and that sort of thing."

"To your knowledge, did Al then make efforts with guides to have your group just be with itself and not with any other stray individuals who might be used to fill the group?"

"Yes, he did. I mean, Al told me on a number of occasions, even on a trip that I wasn't on, that he made it a point that he didn't want anybody else except his group on the trip."

Collins, then, was absolutely adamant in his testimony that no one forced Jim Fasules to join the raft trip down the Chilko. Debra Davy continued the questioning.

"Can you think of anything that prevented Jim Fasules from asking Ron Thompson about the safety of the trip while you were there?"

"No, ma'am," replied Collins.

"Did he seem to you to be a sensible adult?"

"Very much so."

"Was Jim Fasules forced onto that raft on Saturday?"

"No, ma'am."

"If you were invited on a trip as a last-minute fill-in and you had any concerns about what was going to occur, would you have an option to go or not to go?"

"Yes, ma'am, I would."

Davy asked, "Did you hear anyone call Mr. Fasules a wimp?"

"No, ma'am."

"Did Jim Fasules ever say, 'I never expected this' as you hit the whitewater?"

"No."

Next occurred a very unusual line of questioning about the assertion of manliness. It was critical that Debra Davy, as defendant's counsel, prove that Fasules went down the river on his own free will and was fully aware of the danger in doing so.

"Should a grown, intelligent man like you or Jim Fasules let a word like 'wimp' cause you to risk your life or safety?" asked Davy.

"No, but as I have tried to make clear, I don't think any of us, including Mr. Fasules, would have been concerned about being called a wimp if we had expressed a concern about whitewater rafting. I used the word 'wimp'—it was not a phrase I heard anyone else use—I used it in trying to speculate why people might have not spoken up if they, indeed, had a safety concern. I do not think that anybody, including Mr. Fasules, had a safety concern. I did not."

"In your opinion, is being called a wimp a valid reason to override a safety concern for you?"

Collins responded, "If somebody called me a wimp, it wouldn't make any difference to me. If I thought something was not safe, I would not do it."

"Do you have any reason to believe that Jim Fasules didn't hold those same views?"

"No."

Davy had no more questions for the witness. Jim Collins then stood up, quietly left the witness stand, and walked out of the courtroom.

# Chapter Seven

Earl Madsen was undoubtedly the defendant's most important witness. In in a sense, he was the *only* disinterested witness in the entire courtroom since both Al Wolfe and Ron Thompson were considered to be biased because they were, for all intents and purposes, representatives of DDB Needham.

As he interrogated Earl Madsen, the defense attorney, Bill Swindal, was trying to prove, first, that Jim Fasules was well aware of the severity of the rapids and dangers that lay ahead and, second, that Fasules had voluntarily "assumed the risk" of the activity he was about to engage in.

After all, Earl Madsen, Joe Morrison, and Richard O'Reilly had been on the Chilko two years earlier, and they talked enthusiastically among the new group of adventurers about the whitewater in Lava Canyon—and particularly the hazards in White Mile—with the others at the Vancouver airport, where they all had gathered before the trip. Jim Fasules was undoubtedly part of that conversation.

Bill Swindal wasted no time proving this through the testimony of Madsen, an attorney and close personal friend of Al Wolfe since college days. "Do you recall any discussion while all of the men were sitting in the bar at the Vancouver airport about the rapids in Lava Canyon on the Chilko River?"

"Yes," replied Madsen, "Dick O'Reilly and I had been with Joe Morrison on the '85 trip, and I remember Dick in particular talking about the river, and the others asked questions about what it was like for those of us who had floated it before."

"Do you recall how it was described?"

"I can recall it being described as kind of a roller-coaster ride, a couple really big holes. In '85, we had stopped to reconnoiter one of the holes and tied the raft up and walked up a talus slope above this big rapids for Ron Thompson to chart the best way through."

"And that was talked about at the Vancouver airport?" asked Swindal.

"We talked about that as being one of the big holes in the river that we were going to go through, and everybody was going to get soaking wet and . . ."

Swindal then turned to a similar discussion that occurred around the campfire on Thursday evening among those who had chosen the rafting option for the day. Again, Jim Fasules was present to hear the stories about the Chilko's whitewater.

Swindal asked Madsen, "Do you recall any discussions at that time among the group about what their activities had been during the day?"

"Yes, I do," said Madsen, "I remember the stories, particularly those of Dick O'Reilly. When they got back from floating Lava Canyon, they were all soaking wet, and Jack Collins and I had built a fire near the bank of the river. It was a very cold, uncomfortable day. When the rafters got back, they were trying to change clothes and get into dry clothes. Dick O'Reilly got changed and came over and was describing to everybody how spectacular the float had been. It was much more spectacular than when he and I and Joe Morrison had floated it in 1985. Everybody said it was a beautiful, very spectacular float. I remember a lot of discussion about that."

"Do you recall any more particular descriptions that were used by the gentlemen who had floated on Thursday as you were gathered around the campfire that night?"

"I can't remember specific words other than it was very spectacular. They had gone through a number of big holes and had been just doused with water. The water was high. I remember Dick O'Reilly saying it was so great, we ought to float again on Friday, as well as on Saturday going out. A lot of discussion about how spectacular it was."

"Was Jim Fasules present during these conversations?" asked Swindal.

Madsen answered, "Yes, we were all standing around the fire and trying to stay warm."

There had been an insinuation that Jim Fasules had somehow been coerced into joining the raft trip. Swindal quickly proceeded to dispel that misconception.

"Did Jim Fasules say anything to you that led you to believe he intended to raft on Saturday?"

"Well, not specifically. Everybody was going to raft on Saturday because that is how you got out. It was known from day one that we would float the Lava Canyon and get out on Saturday and then go back to Vancouver," Madsen replied.

"And everyone knew the plan was that the rafting would occur on Saturday, correct?"

"That is my understanding."

"Was everyone required to raft on Saturday?" asked Swindal.

"What do you mean 'required'?" inquired Madsen for clarification.

"Well, did you have to get in the raft? Was there any other way other than getting into the raft?"

Madsen replied, "Well, on Saturday morning, we had fished a little, and we were told to pack up all of our gear and the gear would go in the trucks and then we would float down the canyon in the rubber raft. We would not have our gear with us."

"Sir, did you understand there to be an option of either getting into the raft or, if you didn't want to raft, to take a van down to the point below the rapids where you would meet?"

"Well, I don't recall any discussion of it. The vans were there with the gear, and if anybody had wanted to leave with the vans, I suppose they could have. I never heard any discussion of anybody about leaving with the vans and the equipment. Everybody was looking forward to rafting the river."

Swindal was quick to emphasize the fact that Jim Fasules expressed his interest in the whitewater of Lava Canyon. "Did you hear anyone express a hesitancy, such as 'I am not sure I want to raft' or 'I don't want to raft'?"

Madsen instantly replied, "No."

"In your discussions with Jim Fasules prior to Saturday, did he tell you how he got invited to the trip?"

"On Thursday, when we were standing around the fire, he and Gene Yovetich were standing together, and I was talking to him. Jim told me that he had heard of this trip while he and Gene were fishing in Montana and that he wouldn't have missed it for anything."

Madsen's account of the trip down Lava Canyon was about to begin, and he told the jury what happened before the group encountered the set of rapids known as White Mile. Swindal asked Madsen to start from the beginning.

"Sir, let's focus on Saturday, August 1, the day of the accident. Why don't you tell the jury, if you will, how Saturday progressed after you stored your gear in the truck and walked down to where the raft was. Would you take us from that point to just before Bidwell rapids?"

"After we stored the gear, we all got into one raft," Madsen replied. "Arthur Zeikel, one of the other guests, wanted to work the oars and pilot the raft. Ron Thompson told him he could do that, and Ron sat next to Arthur on the big white ice chest. It was very placid for the first section, and Ron had Arthur rowing until we docked the boat to check everything out before going down Lava Canyon. I don't recall much except Arthur Zeikel rowing and everybody giving him advice on what to do."

"What was going on with the others in the raft? Were you just sitting there looking at the birds or talking?" asked Swindal.

"We were having the time of our lives. Everybody was having a great time and really looking forward to going down the rapids and razzing one another as we went along."

"Then you got to the point above Bidwell rapids where the raft was beached, correct?"

"Yes," said Madsen.

"If you would, please describe for the jury the activities that occurred while the raft was beached and just before it left to go into Bidwell rapids."

"We stopped to have a lunch. I recall we had crackers and a very light lunch. And then Ron Thompson spent most of the time checking the gear. I remember he pumped up the raft. He had a foot pump or a hand pump that he used to pump the raft. We were all anxious to get going down the river, and the first person into the boat was Dick O'Reilly, and he chose the right-at-the-front part of the rubber raft. I was getting in next, and Ron Thompson came over and told Dick that he couldn't sit in the front. He would have to sit on the bench seat, which was three or four feet back spanning the sides of the raft. And then we started to fill in where we were going to sit. And there was a lot of discussion of who wanted to ride in the front, which is a little more spectacular because you go nose into the holes and the water comes over. But everybody would be thoroughly doused before we got through."

The life jacket check by Thompson went to the heart of plaintiff's allegation that the life jackets were not properly fitted. Swindal was eager to clear up the record.

"Did you notice any change in Ron Thompson's behavior when you beached the raft before Bidwell rapids?"

"Well, he was very busy checking on the raft, checking on the people. I remember he checked life vests, he checked mine," replied Madsen.

"What do you mean by check? Did he come up and grab it?"

"Well, yes, he came up and grabbed and pulled and made sure that I tightened my ties. I think he was generally having everybody check the life vests they were wearing and made sure that the raft was ready, and then he spent quite a bit of time trying to balance the weight in the raft, the front and the back, and who was going to be seated where."

Madsen then maintained that Thompson gave the group explicit safety instructions in the form of where each one should sit in the raft and how to hold on to the rowing frame and perimeter line around the raft. This testimony, it should be noted, was a much different story than the one provided by Jack Collins, who said that Thompson gave no instructions whatsoever. Bill Swindal hammered home this point of discrepancy.

"Then Ron had each of you sit in a designated location and you proceeded towards Bidwell rapids?"

Madsen responded, "Yeah. Now there was a blue metal rowing frame that spanned across the raft. And then there was a rope on the inside of the raft that went all the way around. When we got into the raft, Ron spent time talking to those of us in the front. And I remember he told me to use my left hand on a rope and put my right hand on the frame."

"Did he give that same instruction to all of you that were sitting in the front of the raft?"

"I don't recall specifically. He kind of spent time with each individual in the front on where they were going to be seated and what they were to hang on to."

Aided by the adroit questions of Bill Swindal, Earl Madsen described the sequence of events leading up to the accident at White Mile. The jury focused on every word as Madsen guided them through the canyon and the intense events of the day.

"Mr. Madsen, would you describe how the raft went through the first big hole or rapid in Bidwell rapids, if you recall?"

"Yes, I recall it. The raft went straight through, nose-first, on the big rapid at Bidwell, and it was very, very solid. I remember we all got very wet in the front, and everybody was yoo-hooing and shouting as we went through. And that was quite a big hole at Bidwell."

"And then, please, if you would, explain to the jury how the trip proceeded thereafter, as you recall it."

"Well, it wasn't very long after we went through the first hole, and we got in the current, and we were floating sideways down the river. From where I was seated, I was looking right straight down the river. And that's when I first saw the rock that we were going to hit. And the current had pulled us into the mainstream, where we were clearly going to run broadside into that rock. And I think I saw it first because I mentioned to Ron that we are going to hit it. I mentioned that to him several times, and he didn't acknowledge me, but I could see from his eyes that he had seen the rock and that he was working the oars as hard as he could to try to pull the boat to the side."

Madsen then explained Thompson's frantic reaction to the impending accident.

"What was Ron Thompson trying to do as you saw it?"

"He was rowing as hard as he could on those oars."

"Which way was he trying to get the boat to go?"

"To back it out of the main current."

"You mean like this [indicating]?"

"Yes. If he had been successful, it would have just backed us . . ."

"It would have gone right around like this [indicating]?"

"Yes. We would have had the back of the boat leading down the river, which is common in rafting, but we wouldn't have gone down sideways."

"He couldn't do that?"

"No, he could not," said Madsen.

"The raft hit the rock like this [indicating]?"

"That's correct."

The collision with the rock in White Mile was inevitable, and Madsen told the jury what occurred next.

"How do you recall what happened then? Which way did the raft go?" asked Swindal.

"The raft hit absolutely in the center and just stopped on the rock."

Swindal wanted clarification.

"Dead in the water?"

"Dead in the water. Ron had jumped down on the front edge of the raft, as he saw we were coming into the rock to push off with his hands. I was totally unconcerned. I had been in many raft situations where we have pushed off rocks and snags. So he was trying to push off the rock with his knee. He was down on one knee on the edge of the front of the raft."

"About where you were sitting? Do you want to come and show the jury? He came off the ice chest?"

"Right. And moved down to this side [indicating], on the side of the rubber raft. As I recall, he had one foot on the floor of the raft and his knee on the side, and he pushed on the raft. He turned around and he said, 'Everybody get to the rock side,' and that was the first time I knew we were in trouble.'"

"The next thing you recall, where were you?" Swindal asked.

Madsen replied, "I was at the bottom of the river. I had no recollection of the raft being anything but perfectly horizontal and stable. I had no sense of the raft tipping or moving, but I just went straight down, and I remember hitting the bottom of the river just like this on my back [indicating]."

"Like a snap of the fingers, and you were on the bottom of . . ."

"Absolutely. I had no idea we were going to have a problem."

Madsen testified that all of the men—with the exception of Collins—quickly fell out of the boat. The jury's attention was riveted on Madsen as he told of his encounter with the river's currents.

"Would you then tell the jury, Mr. Madsen, what happened to you after you found yourself on the bottom of the river?" Swindal asked.

"Well, the first thing that happened was that the river rolled me down the river head over heels on the bottom of the river, and then the life vest pulled me up, and I came up underneath the raft. I could feel the raft, but the bottom of the raft was black. The raft was so large it shut out any of the light. So I didn't know where I was. I tried to reach around the raft to see if I was in the front or the edge, but all I could feel was the bottom of the raft, and then the current took me back down again."

"Did you come up again?"

"The same thing happened. It rolled me head over heels on the bottom of the river, and I came up again, and the same thing happened."

"Then what happened? Did you go back down for the third time as they say?"

"Yes, I went down the third time, and I was totally out of air."

"Then what happened?"

"Then my vest pulled me up, and this time I could see I was out from under the raft. I could see the white bubbles in the water, which I knew to be the surface of the river. So I just kicked as hard as I could to try to get up to the surface and to get far enough out of the water so that I could try to handle the raft if it came over the top of me again."

"When you came to the surface, you were no longer under the raft, right?"

"No, I came out of the surface in front of the raft, and I came out very vigorously out of the water. I came clear out up to my chest—up to my armpits—and I had my arms as high up as I could reach because I was afraid that raft would come right over me. Sure enough, it did."

"Did you grab onto it?"

"Yes."

"Who was in the raft, if anybody?"

"At the time I didn't know there was anybody in the raft, but very shortly after that I found out that Jack Collins was in there."

"The raft was still upright at the time?"

"Yes."

"Did you try to get into the raft?"

"Yes. The first thing I remember is Jack Collins grabbed my life vest and was trying to pull me in, but the life vest just slid up and got in my face, and I was having a great deal of difficulty breathing because as he pulled on my vest, he choked off my air supply. So I just beat his arms off and told him to leave it alone."

"And you were there on the outside of the raft and hanging on as the raft was going through the rapids?"

"Yes, initially, I was in the front, and the first thing I tried to do was kick free of the raft and get away from the raft because it was my biggest problem, I thought. And just then we started going through all of the rapids, and then I decided it was better to hang on to the raft than to let go, and that is what I did."

"Was the raft eventually beached somewhere?"

"Yes."

Collins's dramatic rescue of Madsen filled the courtroom with the same sense of dread that those on the Chilko must have experienced. Swindal was artful in his handling of the interrogation.

"And what happened at that point?"

Madsen replied, "Jack had told me that there was an eddy and that if I could let go of the raft, I would probably float to the shore. And so I let go, and the current drifted me to the shore, and I had no feeling in my arms or in my hands then. So, I remember grabbing the rocks underneath with my knees to keep the current from pulling me back down, and I just kind of rolled on my side there. And within a few minutes I got up on the beach. Jack had by that time tied the boat up just a short distance downstream, maybe 20 or 25 yards, and he came back, and he had a knife, and he cut the strings on my vinyl hooded jacket that had been severely knotted. So he just cut that off and got my clothes off because I was starting to get hypothermia at that point. And he took my parka and my sweatshirt off. I had a sweatshirt on and a parka. And then he just used his body to warm me up there momentarily."

"And then you and Jack Collins climbed up the ledge to where the road was?" Swindal asked.

"That is right. Well, there was no road. The road was on the other side of the river, and I remember, after Jack cut the jacket off, sitting on a rock in the sun. This was the first day we had any sun on the whole trip, and I remember just sitting up on the rock and getting warm and then deciding that we better start hiking out. I knew where we were."

Swindal seemed surprised. "You knew where you were?"

"Yes. I knew that we could hike down to the juncture of the Taseko and the Chilko River and that that would be where the camp was and they would have rafts down there. It is a huge campsite area, and that there would be no problem."

"Did you have any concerns about being able to get to that campsite at the junction before dark?"

"No," replied Madsen.

"Sir, were you injured?"

"Yes."

"What were your injuries?"

"I had broken ribs and a lacerated kidney and quite a few bone chips here and there."

And then Swindal asked Madsen the blockbuster of a question.

"Would you go down this river again with Ron Thompson?"

"Yes."

Swindal then moved the dialogue with Earl Madsen to the important issue of the legal liability of Needham as the organizer of the trip as opposed to Thompson, the outfitter who actually conducted the activities.

"Mr. Madsen, what did you understand to be Al Wolfe's role in connection with the 1987 Chilko trip?"

"Well, Al arranged the trip and the schedules—he arranged for the guide, corresponded with us as to where we would meet and when and how we would take the trip."

"Who was in charge of running the trip on the Chilko River on August 1, 1987?" Swindal asked.

"On the river, Ron Thompson was in charge. He had the gear, all of the equipment, and he was in charge of everything on the river."

"Mr. Madsen, at any time during the trip when you were in the Chilko River area, did you ever hear Al Wolfe make any statements to Ron Thompson as to how many rafts to use on this trip?"

"Did I hear him make my statements to Ron? No."

"Did you hear Al Wolfe say to Ron Thompson, 'You are not to use two rafts—you are to use one raft'?"

"No, I remember on Saturday that Al was very upset that we were going to use one raft instead of two."

"What did Al Wolfe say? Do you remember?"

Madsen replied, "He just came by and made a comment to me that this was a complete surprise to him—that Ron had one raft—and that we were supposed to have two."

"Was there any discussion, that you were part of, about the fact that there was one raft—among the participants, I mean?"

"No. The only question was whether there was room for everybody, and then I think Ron Thompson said, 'This is no problem' and 'There is plenty of room.'"

No doubt feeling confident about the reassuring testimony that Madsen had provided, Swindal concluded his questioning of Madsen.

Brian Crowe then began his cross-examination. The result, unfortunately for the defendant, was a devastating exchange about a lack of safety instructions given by Thompson regarding self-rescue, throw ropes, and pulling a swimmer back into the raft. In an artful exchange, Crowe revealed his well-deserved reputation.

"Did Ron Thompson, before you got in that boat, give you any safety instructions with the other men at the put-in point?"

"Not that I recall," Madsen replied.

"And, sir, isn't it a fact that you were given some safety instructions in 1985? Isn't that right?"

"I'm sure we were."

"And in 1985. do you recall Thompson instructing you that if you fell out of the raft you were to lay on your back and try to get to the shore?"

"I can't recall when I received that instruction, but I remember that in '87. That's what several of us were discussing before we got into the raft above Bidwell Rapids."

"Isn't it a fact, sir, that you only heard one person in the boat say something about that?" Crowe inquired.

"Well, I remember it being discussed, but I can't remember what the circumstance was now. But I remember it being discussed—that if you fall out, put your feet down and stay on your back."

"And you heard that discussed by one of the other invitees in the boat, isn't that right?"

"Yes."

The accomplished attorney that he was, Crowe did not let the opportunity pass. "Ron Thompson never told that you in 1987, did he, sir?"

"No, that was discussed by one of the other guests in the boat."

"And you never heard Ron Thompson say anything about how to rescue someone with a throw rope if they fell out of the raft?"

"No."

"You never heard Ron Thompson talk about how to pull someone back into to the raft by their life jacket if they fell into the river?"

"No."

"And you really didn't hear Ron Thompson give any safety instructions in 1987, isn't that right, sir?" Crowe persisted.

"Well, I considered them safety instructions—the instructions that he told us in the front of the boat."

"Oh, you mean when you were in the boat?"

"Yes, before we were in the current," said Madsen.

Brian Crowe clarified the question. "Hold on to the rope with one hand and the metal frame with the other hand?"

"Well, he checked our life vests . . . ," responded Madsen.

"Let's talk about what Thompson told you, okay?"

"Okay."

"He said hold on to the rope with one hand and the metal frame with the other hand, is that right?"

"Uh-huh."

"And that's all the instructions he gave you, isn't that?"

"On that, yes," Madsen reluctantly admitted.

Then came the critical issue regarding the weight of the raft, which the plaintiff claimed was overloaded. In a word, Crowe drew blood while making a number of devastating points.

"Sir, isn't it a fact that the weight of the boat interfered with the ability of Thompson to maneuver it out of the way?"

"I assumed that it did."

"And isn't that the reason that you could not get the raft past the rock?" Crowe asked.

"I assumed that Thompson could not because—with the weight of the people in the boat—he could not row it and move it into the current."

"And that was my next question—did the weight of the boat and the number of people in it affect its maneuverability?"

"I think it did. I assumed that it did," responded Madsen.

When the questioning ceased, Madsen had done well in his direct examination, but his cross-examination could not have been welcomed by the defense team. This was a perfect example of the fact that a trial is a precarious and unpredictable beast, and its course can quickly take a turn for the worse.

# Chapter Eight

Next to take the witness stand was Al Wolfe, the originator and organizer of the Needham-sponsored raft trip down the Chilko River. It is no exaggeration to say that Wolfe's testimony was widely anticipated by everyone in the courtroom.

To avoid liability, Needham, as the defendant, had to prove that Wolfe had merely organized the trip—and that he had nothing to do with its actual operation, particularly the critical decision to take only one boat. To set the stage, the defendant's attorney, Bill Swindal, first asked Wolfe about the business purpose behind the trip.

"Sir, you are the person who organized the 1987 Chilko trip, aren't you?"

"Right."

"What was the purpose of that trip?"

"Well, the purpose of that trip—and all of them—started with a business base. You know, I had a responsibility for building the Chicago office, and in the advertising business—if I get too far astray here, stop me."

"We will," replied Swindal.

"In the advertising business, you either have to grow or dry up. You know, your current clients are more attracted to you because they see you succeed with new business, and it feeds the momentum of the agency. So we had to do two things. We had to grow our existing business, and we had to attract new business. And I always felt philosophically that you didn't get new business by wining and dining. Frankly, that just wasn't my bag. I do not think I brought more than two or three people into my home for business entertainment. If clients were in town, I was out of there at 6:30 or 7:00 and wasn't staying for dinner."

"Now, getting back to this point—what was the reason?" asked Swindal.

"I felt that if you had good people working for you and you are turning out a good product, the more you can expose those employees to clients and prospects, the better chance you have of making their list if they ever decide to move a piece of business or add an agency. When I put these trips together, I thought it was a way to cut through all of the trappings and titles and get our employees with clients where they could really get to know them and that respect and positive feelings would develop."

Swindal asked Wolfe to explain how he selected the Chilko River as the destination for his next client development effort. "I would like to bring your attention now to the Chilko River trips that you organized. Would you tell the jury how you found Ron Thompson for the 1985 Chilko trip?"

"Well, it starts with a basic premise that whenever I put one of these trips together, I had to make sure that we do it for a limited period of time because of all these busy schedules that people had, trying to bring anywhere about a dozen of those people together and do it for no more than five or six days, including travel time, was just impossible. The Selway River worked because it was one we could do four days on the river, a day in and a day out. People could stretch, but they could accommodate that. We took one run on the Middle Fork of the Salmon—I think that was a six-day trip—and you know, it was just pushing the calendar too much. So we went back to the Selway. We couldn't get on the Selway for the '85 trip, so I started to look for something else in approximately that time range."

When the Selway was unavailable, Wolfe was told by the outfitter and the booking agency that he should look into the Chilko River in British Columbia and the outfitter, Ron Thompson.

Swindal asked, "Did you speak with Ron Thompson by phone?"

"Yes, I did," replied Wolfe.

"And do you recall that conversation?"

"Well, you know, there were several conversations over a period of years, but that initial conversation was, 'Look, I would like to put a group together so that we can have, you know, kind of our own private group out there, folks that just want to get away from all of the hassle and congestion and confusion of the day-to-day job. Do you think that you can handle a group like that, and can we get in and out of there in a period of about five days, including flight time?' Thompson said, 'Absolutely,' and he talked about the Taseko and the Chilko rivers."

"Did you then go up and visit Mr. Thompson?" asked Swindal.

"I did. I flew up for a meeting with Ron and met him at Williams Lake, and he had a pilot there that he arranged, and we then flew out over parts of the Taseko and Chilko."

"Did you have a further discussion with Ron Thompson when you were flying over the river?"

"Well, I had further conversations with him in the plane. He described some of what we were going over."

Swindal asked, "What were you looking for in Ron Thompson when you went to interview him and fly over the river?"

"I was looking for someone I felt we could rely on. Someone, you know, who knew the outdoor business and knew rafting—that we could count on to, you know, carry through and do the job."

"Did Mr. Thompson explain to you his experience on the Chilko River?"

Wolfe replied, "Thompson said, 'I don't think there is anyone that has more experience on the Chilko than I do.' And he had taken a sizable number of trips, and I asked him if he had had any accidents, and he said, 'No.' And I came out of that with a general feeling of comfort—that the guy knew what he was doing. The Chilko was an interesting alternative—that didn't chew up a lot of time—to the Selway River. And you know, it was worth taking a crack at."

Wolfe explained his decision to return to the Chilko two years later with Thompson as the outfitter.

"And you went with Ron Thompson on the 1985 trip?"

"Yes, we did.

"When it came time to plan the 1987 trip, what did you do?"

"I went back to Steve Currey to see if there was a possibility that we could go back on the Selway again, and Steve said, 'I am not running it regularly now and it would be tough at this point to block that out.' So from there, I thought, 'Well, I'll go back to Ron and see if there is a way for us to work a trip out that does not include the Taseko.' And his solution was, 'Hey, we can get good rafting on the Lava Canyon and good fishing in that area, and we can work out a combination over three days so that people can do what they want to the first couple of days, and then we'll float out together the third day.'"

"And you decided to go with Ron Thompson in 1987?"

"Yes, I did. We had a very enjoyable trip in '85, and there was nothing in that trip to lead us to question Ron Thompson."

Wolfe was asked about his decision to invite Jim Fasules on the trip. This testimony was important because it went to Fasules's knowledge concerning the hazards of the river—and whether he had knowingly and willingly "assumed the risk" of the rapids in Lava Canyon. Wolf described the initial phone call to Fasules at his second home in Montana.

"There came a time, Mr. Wolfe, where you decided to extend an invitation to Jim Fasules to go on the 1987 trip, did you not?"

"That's right."

"When did you make the decision that you would invite Jim on the trip?"

"Well, it was in late July."

"Do you recall making the invitation?"

"Yes, I do. I extended the invitation through Gene Yovetich, who was joining us on the Chilko and who happened to be out with Jim fishing in Montana."

"Where was Gene Yovetich when you called him?" asked Swindal.

"Gene Yovetich was in the area; I think it was around Ennis, Montana, where the Fasules family had a cabin."

"And would you tell the jury what was said in that telephone conversation?"

"I said, 'Gene, we have got an opening on the trip. Do you think Jim Fasules would like to join us?' And Gene said, 'Are you kidding?' He said, 'Let me talk to him.' And he did, and then Jim called back."

At the prompting of Bill Swindal, Al Wolfe continued his testimony. "Did you receive a subsequent telephone conversation about the invitation to James Fasules?"

"I got a call from Jim, yes."

"And where were you when you received the call?"

"I was in my office in Chicago."

"Was anyone else on the phone other than you and James."

"My secretary, Mary Kaban."

"All right. Sir, do you recall that telephone conversation?"

"Generally, yes."

"All right. Please tell us as best as you can recall what you said to James Fasules and what James Fasules said to you."

"Okay. You know, Mary Kahan said, 'Jim Fasules is on the phone,' and I picked up and said, 'Hello, Jim. How are things in Montana?' He said, 'Good.' He said, 'Do you still have an opening?' And I said, 'We sure do. Would you like to go?' And he said, 'You bet.' I said, 'Have you had a chance to talk to Gene?' He said, 'Yes.' I said, 'Jim, it should be a great trip. We would love to have you.' I said, 'It will be at least 45 minutes of the wildest and woolliest whitewater that I have been on, and I think we ought to be able to get some good rainbow trout fishing in, too.' I said, 'If there are any details that you need on this, Mary is on the other line, and she can provide them for you.' I said, 'I'm really pleased you're going, I think you will enjoy it, and we would love having you.' And that was the end of my conversation."

"Sir, after that telephone conversation, did you have any other discussions with James Fasules about the rafting portion of the 1987 trip?" asked Swindal.

"Prior to Vancouver or . . ."

"At any time after that telephone conversation you just described for us?"

"Yes, I did."

"And when did that occur?"

"There was a conversation that took place in Vancouver that a number of people were participating in, and Dick O'Reilly and some of the others who had been on the prior trip were talking about Lava Canyon and their experience in it."

"Were you there?"

"I was there for part of it, and then I was out for part of it because there were stragglers coming in."

"All right. Were you present, and was James Fasules present?"

"Yes."

"Where did that discussion take place?"

"It was a restaurant near the Vancouver airport terminal where people were having a sandwich and a beer."

And then, according to Wolfe, there were two other conversations with Jim Fasules about the rapids of Lava Canyon.

Swindal asked, "Did you have a subsequent conversation or discussion with James Fasules in which rafting the Lava Canyon was discussed?"

"Yes."

"When did that occur?"

Wolfe replied, "I had two. Let's take the first one. The first one was after we had come back on Thursday, the first day, when we had split the group. Some people were rafting down Lava Canyon, and some stayed to fish. The non-fisherman—I think there were five of us—went down the Chilko. When we came back, Jim happened to ask Stu Sharpe and myself, you know, what it was like. I said from my standpoint it was wet and colder than hell. We had no sun that day, and I was just shaking like a leaf. The float itself was terrific, but normally when you get splashed from the waves and everything, you have some sun to dry you out. We didn't have sun that day, and it was really cold. Then he asked Stu, and Stu made some comments about how it was a great run, but it was cold."

"Did Jim Fasules say anything to either yourself or Mr. Sharpe at that time?" asked Swindal.

"He just asked us, you know, about our experience, and he listened, and that was the extent of it."

And there was a subsequent conversation with Jim Fasules that Al Wolfe said he would never forget. "You said there was a second time after that when you had a conversation with James Fasules concerning the rafting of Lava Canyon. When did that occur?" Swindal asked.

"That occurred on Saturday before we got in the raft to go down through Lava Canyon."

"Do you recall the conversation?"

"Yes, I do. That will be with me the rest of my life."

"Would you tell the jury what that conversation was?"

"I said, 'Jim, this is going to be the thrill of a lifetime.'"

"Did Mr. Fasules say anything in return?"

"He just smiled at me."

The testimony then moved to the critical question concerning the use of only one raft.

"Mr. Wolfe, did you tell Ron Thompson on Saturday or at any other time how many rafts to use on this trip?"

"Of course not," replied Wolfe.

"Did you tell Ron Thompson on Saturday or at any other time how the raft trip should be operated through Lava Canyon?"

"I did not."

"Did you interfere with Ron Thompson in the operation of the trip through Lava Canyon in any way?"

"No, I didn't."

"Did you pressure Ron Thompson to do something he didn't want?"

"No, I did not."

"Were you present at the riverside on Saturday morning as the trip was about to load into the raft and go down the Chilko?" asked Swindal.

"Yes, I was."

"Do you recall anyone saying at that time, 'I don't want to go'?"

"No," said Wolfe.

Interestingly enough, Swindal did not ask Al Wolfe about any earlier conversations with Thompson to make the group "exclusive."

Then came the critical line of questioning about Thompson's safety instructions. Wolfe testified that there was a discussion about keeping your feet in front of you if you fell into the river, about "high siding" should the raft hit a boulder in the river, about holding on to the boat in whitewater, and about Thompson's checking everyone's life jacket. Wolfe's testimony contrasted noticeably with that of Earl Madsen, who stated that there were no instructions other than to hold on. And certainly, Wolfe's testimony differed from that given by Jack Collins, who claimed that there were no safety instructions at all.

Swindal wanted Wolfe to clear up the discrepancy.

"Sir, do you recall on Saturday any safety instructions that were given by Ron Thompson?"

"Yes, I do," replied Wolfe.

"What do you recall, and when were the instructions given?"

"I was a little bit tuned out, but there were some instructions that Thompson gave initially on Saturday that 'if anything happens and you go into the water, keep your feet ahead of you.' I remember very specifically the later instructions because I was focused on those a lot more, but I think his routine at the time was to take it beyond that a talk about 'if we hit something and I holler, "Go to the high side, go to the high side fast.'" He very specifically told us that when we made our stop later that day and before we started into the White Mile."

"Sir, are you telling us there were safety instructions given two times on Saturday?" Swindal asked.

"Yes, but with a lot more urgency before we went into the White Mile," Wolfe stated.

"Was that the second time?" asked Swindal.

"The second time, right."

"That is when the craft was beached?"

"Yes, Thompson pulled us over to the side. We all took care of personal matters there, and Thompson personally checked everyone's life vests at that point to see if they were all right. And he talked to us about how to hold on in the rapids. He told us to make sure that you really held on to those ropes, and there was a metal rod in a couple of spots mounted over the raft. And then he went into the thing about, 'If you go in, get those feet out in front of you so that it protects the rest of your body.' And he said, 'If we hit anything, I am going to yell, and you are going to have to move fast.' And that was what he said."

So there it was—Wolfe had testified that there was a complete safety briefing from Thompson covering all the important issues of self-rescue and high siding, especially before entering the rapids at White Mile. Wolfe's testimony was at odds with that of Collins and Madsen, who stated that Thompson never mentioned how to swim rapids or execute a high-side maneuver.

# Chapter Nine

A large part of any plaintiff's wrongful death case is the choice of expert witnesses retained to prove the negligence of the defendant. To illuminate exactly what went wrong on the Chilko River that dreadful day, the plaintiff hired a well-respected whitewater safety expert named Les Bechdel, who was without question one of the top authorities in the field.

For a decade, Bechdel had worked as a kayak instructor for the Nantahala Outdoor Center, universally considered the Harvard of paddling schools. And he was the coauthor of the book *River Rescue* with Slim Ray in 1985, still considered one of the standard references for river safety and rescue. Bechdel had also founded the company Canyons, Inc., a rafting outfitter with operations on the Main and Middle forks of the Salmon River deep in the wilderness regions of Idaho.

Bechdel's testimony was at times heavily scripted and often overly harsh in its assessment of Thompson's operations. Interestingly, many of the criticisms leveled against Thompson were not followed by Bechdel in his own outfitting business. It was also no coincidence that the plaintiff's counsel, Brian Crowe, had Bechdel compare the Chilko to the relatively mild Main Salmon River—not the more dangerous Middle Fork, which is a true millrace that at certain water levels is considered as dangerous as the Chilko if not more so.

Naturally, Bechdel explained any distinctions away by saying that the Chilko is a much more difficult river than the Main Salmon. Nonetheless, after Bechdel's testimony, the jury most certainly began to question the competency of Thompson, particularly as regarded his decision to take only one boat (and no safety kayak) but also Thompson's lack of detailed safety talks to the passengers and perhaps even his failure to provide them with wetsuits, helmets, and additional throw ropes.

When Crowe asked Bechdel to render an overall evaluation of Thompson's operations, Bechdel cut him up into small pieces and spared him absolutely no mercy.

Crowe bluntly asked Bechdel, "What are your opinions concerning the conduct of Ron Thompson in this case?"

"I felt that he did not provide enough warnings to the participants in this tragedy. I felt his instructions and his educational efforts were inadequate. I felt his equipment was inadequate. I felt that he succumbed to pressure from Mr. Wolfe that caused him to run a one-raft trip. I think his safety plan and the risk management attentions weren't very good."

Crowe asked Bechdel about the number of people on the raft that day, and Bechdel's reply was unusually terse.

"What are your opinions concerning the safety plan that Ron Thompson had on August 1, 1987?"

"Well, taking this many people down in one raft was absolutely insane. I mean you have to understand that this raft is about 18 feet long, eight feet wide, and it's controlled by a set of oars that Mr. Thompson had. He had six men in the front and five in the back, and the lightest one was maybe 200 pounds. I mean that is an incredible amount of weight that you have to control while you descend this river, avoiding all these obstacles and hazards that we discussed this afternoon. Overcoming that weight—once that raft starts traveling in one direction—you are overcoming a lot of inertia to change that direction and get it steering again in a different way. And the other factor is that weight is at the ends of the boat, which was what we call swing weight phenomenon. Once that weight starts swinging in a circular fashion, it exacerbates the problem."

"From the standpoint of maneuverability of the raft?"

"Yes, it's much harder to maneuver with that many people in the raft."

"Mr. Bechdel, assume for the moment that the weight of everybody in that raft taken together met the standards for the weight capacity of that particular raft. Was that raft still overcrowded?"

"Yes. The raft may have met some capacity measurement for floating in flat water, but it's the control that was lost by piling all those people in that raft."

Crowe asked Bechdel about the weight of the raft as it related to the high-siding maneuver. "What about as it relates to high siding; how does the crowding of the raft affect high siding?"

"I mean physically you couldn't do it. I mean it's just too crowded for all 12 bodies to get on to the high side. And that is why I believe the raft went up on edge so far. The guys on the left side of the raft couldn't get to the high side because three people were already there in front of them—if the maneuver was ever even tried."

"And did you see any evidence that the overloading of the raft actually affected Thompson's ability to control the raft?"

"Yes, in Madsen's deposition, he talks about Thompson's inability to control the raft because the people in the front kept leaning back and hitting the oars. Thompson couldn't take effective strokes to control the boat."

Crowe continued to prompt Bechdel in what was obviously a well-rehearsed presentation. Oddly enough, counsel for defendant never objected on the grounds that the witness was being led by the plaintiff's lawyer.

Crowe continued. "All right. What other aspects of Thompson's safety plan were inadequate in your mind, Mr. Bechdel?"

"Well, we have discussed a little bit about this rope-throwing concept. And part of my safety plan—God forbid if I ever ran a single-raft trip like that—would be to employ these van drivers that just twiddle their thumbs somewhere and have them set up a rope at Bidwell Rapids. I would run Bidwell and then eddy out and give them a chance to get back to the van and drive on down to White Mile at the bottom and set up a rope there too."

"Okay. Now, these are the same van drivers you are paying to pick up the people at the Taseko junction anyway, right?" asked Crowe.

"Exactly."

"So it's not more expensive to have Mr. Thompson to have those guys stationed at the bottom of Bidwell or at the bottom of White Mile, is it?"

"No, it would be a good use of their manpower."

"And those van drivers could be used to throw ropes, right, to the people?"

"They could arrive ahead of the raft, walk down there, and have a couple throw-rope stations along the shore. And then once you ran Bidwell, you would eddy out, have a little snack, take a break. And then they could jump in the van, drive on down at the bottom of White Mile where the road is close to the river."

At first, Bechdel stated on the stand that safety kayakers would have been "helpful," but after Crowe nudged him a bit, he changed his testimony to state that safety kayakers were in fact a "necessity." The exchange, needless to say, made Bechdel look malleable.

"What else about the safety plan? You talked about the one-raft trip. What else?" asked Crowe.

"Well, the obvious thing is you never want to raft alone. You want to have multiple rafts. Safety kayakers would have been a great thing to have on a river like this. They park themselves—you know, run the rapids ahead of time, set up ropes to get out of the kayak, and set up throw ropes where they could be on hand in case after somebody fell out."

"Okay. I don't want to talk, however, Mr. Bechdel, about what is in the abstract. You say 'would have been a great thing to have.' The question is, should Thompson have had a safety kayak on this trip?"

"Thompson should have had a safety kayak. He should have had a second raft," said Bechdel.

"And that is what you would have done if you ran this river in 1987?"

"You bet your bottom dollar."

Crowe asked Bechdel about the difficulty of the river. "To rehash, Mr. Bechdel, it's your opinion that this is Class V whitewater?"

"That's correct. Again, Class V whitewater poses significant hazards."

"Do you mean to say that the Lava Canyon section of the Chilko River should not be commercially run?" asked Crowe.

"No, I am not saying that. I think it can be commercially run," said Bechdel.

"Under what conditions should it be commercially run?" asked Crowe.

"Well, I would certainly have more than one raft going down a time. I would run a safety kayaker. I would have wetsuits on my people and helmets on them."

Crowe then had Les Bechdel agree that the Chilko was not only a *dangerous* river but also an *inherently dangerous* river. Then, in an interesting turn of events (and one probably not anticipated by Crowe), Bechdel responded that practically *any* river is "inherently dangerous." Bechdel asserted that even in the absence of wrongdoing, a person could be injured on a gentle river.

Bechdel's admission seemed to negate any negligence on Thompson's part. If all rivers are inherently dangerous and accidents can happen anywhere without wrongdoing by the outfitter, how could Thompson be held responsible for the death of Jim Fasules?

Crowe moved quickly to try to explain Bechdel's faux pas. "Mr. Bechdel, do you believe this is a dangerous river?"

"I do."

"Do you believe this is an inherently dangerous river?" asked Crowe.

"I believe it is inherently dangerous," replied Bechdel.

"Mr. Bechdel, do you believe that the Main Salmon River which you were running in 1986 and 1987 was also inherently dangerous?"

"Yes."

"Do you believe that the Lava Canyon section of the Chilko River was *more* dangerous?"

"Yes," replied Bechdel.

"Now, when you say inherently dangerous, what does that mean in your mind?"

"Well, once you get to grade III and up, I mean there is definitely a chance you are going to fall out. And it gets worse the higher you go up in the rating system. The consequences of injury are greater when you fall out of a boat."

Strangely enough, Crowe's further line of questioning tended to exculpate the defendant.

"You are not saying it is not possible that you could be injured on a Class II river, are you?"

"Yes, you would have to work at it, but, yes, you could hurt yourself on a Class II river."

"You are saying even in the absence of wrongdoing, someone could be hurt on the Main Salmon River in Idaho?"

"Yep. You bet."

Then there was the most remarkable question of all.

"You are saying the same thing on the Lava Canyon section of Chilko River that it is so dangerous that even in the absence of wrongdoing, someone could be injured?"

"That's right," stated Bechdel.

During Bechdel's testimony, a number of interesting sidebars occurred between the judge and junior associate Phillip Goldberg, an attorney for the plaintiff. One of these conversations between judge and counsel got a little contentious. The court remarked—clearly tongue in cheek—with an oblique reference to the rating of rapids, and Goldberg reacted defensively. This response violated the first rule of courtroom etiquette—the judge is always right. From the trial transcript:

MR. GOLDBERG: Judge, I would like a sidebar, if possible.

THE COURT: All right.

MR. GOLDBERG: Judge, I cite to the court *Ponder vs. Warren Tool Corp.*, which is a 10th Circuit opinion, and it basically says that testimony material and . . .

THE COURT: Go slower and quieter.

MR. GOLDBERG: Regarding cause . . .

THE COURT: You sound like a Class V lawyer.

MR. GOLDBERG: I sound like a young, innovative lawyer.

With that awkward exchange behind them, Crowe proceeded apace with his questioning of Bechdel about the safety of always taking another boat on the river.

"Mr. Bechdel, is it more probably true than not that a second raft, had it been on this trip, could have picked Jim Fasules out of the water?"

"Yes, it is more probably true."

"Is it more probably true than not true that a safety kayaker could have ferried Jim Fasules to the side of the river to safety?"

"Yes, it is probably true."

Crowe then delved into what he perceived as deficiencies of safety gear provided by Ron Thompson as the outfitter.

"What equipment should have been required on this trip?"

"The participants should have had wetsuits and helmets."

"And why should they have had wetsuits?"

"A wetsuit would have reduced the chances of developing immersion hypothermia—getting cold. It would have kept them warm. A wetsuit also provides padding. If you do bang into a rock, you have foam there to protect you from injury or reduce the amount of injury. It provides less drag. If you have to swim in rapids with clothing on, there is a lot of drag. And, finally, it is extra floatation. It is more floatation in addition to the life jackets they were wearing."

"Okay. Directing your attention to McGinnis's book, *Class V Briefing*, what does he say about wetsuits?" asked Crowe.

"Wetsuits are essential," replied Bechdel.

Crowe concluded his direct examination of Les Bechdel as an expert witness on behalf of the plaintiff. On cross-examination, the defendant's attorney, Bill Swindal, proceeded to impugn the credibility of Bechdel by showing hypocrisy in Bechdel's own whitewater rafting operations. For a lawyer, there is no greater pleasure than exposing hypocrisy in the courtroom, and Swindal clearly relished the exchange.

"Now, Mr. Bechdel, it is okay for you to sit here and say that wetsuits should have been required. But did you require wetsuits for your participants in 1987?" asked Swindal.

"Nope, I didn't," admitted Bechdel.

"Why is that, Mr. Bechdel?"

"Well, the river I am running is a lot easier than the Chilko River. It is a Class III and Class IV river on the Main Salmon. It's a pool-and-drop river. The amount of time that somebody would fall out of one of my rafts on one of my trips would be maybe five minutes, maybe six minutes. They are not exposed to the risks like they had in the Chilko. And my river, what is called a deep-water river, it is a bigger volume, and there is less rocks near the surface than what you see on the Chilko."

Swindal moved quickly to expose Bechdel's hypocrisy by showing that Bechdel did not follow his own advice regarding helmets either.

"Now, let's go back to the helmets issue. You believe helmets should have been required?" Swindal asked.

"That's right," said Bechdel.

"Take a look at McGinnis's book. What does he say there about helmets?

"'Helmets. All Class V paddle crews wear helmets, no exceptions. Helmets not only protect paddlers should they go overboard, they also diminish the chance of injury from clanging heads or whaps to the noggin by paddle handles.'"

"When you say 'paddle crews,' that doesn't relate to just the guides, does it?" asked Swindal.

"No, that is the people in the raft, everybody," Bechdel said.

"Mr. Bechdel, again did you provide helmets to your passengers in 1987?"

"No, I didn't."

"Why is that?"

"The Main Salmon isn't full of violent rapids. It doesn't have the kind of force that you see on the Chilko. I mean the chance of falling out is less. And if you do, like I said I before, there are not as many rocks in the Main Salmon."

In his testimony before the court, Bechdel seemed to contradict himself when he said that the victims in the present case would have lived if they had been wearing wetsuits and helmets but then acknowledged that there were rafting fatalities in Canada in which the paddlers were wearing wetsuits and helmets.

"Did you focus on any other accidents that occurred in Canada prior to 1987?" asked Swindal.

"There was one on the Elaho River where people got caught up on a logjam, and they were wearing wetsuits," admitted Bechdel.

"Okay. When was that?"

"1987, I think July 1."

Swindal noted, "Just a month before this accident, wasn't it?"

"Yes," conceded Bechdel.

"Did you look at any other accidents, Mr. Bechdel, that occurred in Canada prior to 1987?"

"There was a drowning in Ontario where a guy was wearing a life jacket, a wetsuit, and a helmet, and he got caught in a hydraulic and drowned, and that was on a commercial raft trip in 1983," said Bechdel, seemingly oblivious to the fact that a wetsuit and helmet failed to protect the victim.

Swindal next moved to the subject of what should be Needham's liability for Jim Fasules's death on the Chilko River.

"Now, Mr. Bechdel, let's move past equipment for a minute and move past instructions. Do you have any opinions concerning the conduct of DDB Needham, the defendant in this case?" Swindal asked.

"Yes, I do."

"What are your opinions, sir?"

"Well, the first thing is they should never have invited Mr. Fasules on this trip."

Swindal asked, "Why is that?"

"Fasules had no experience. He had never done any whitewater before. In fact, he didn't even—he didn't even think it was going to be a whitewater trip. He thought it was going to be a fishing trip."

"Assuming there was proof that Fasules had never been whitewater rafting, you are saying if someone hasn't been whitewater rafting before, you shouldn't go in the Lava Canyon?"

"You don't take a novice to Lava Canyon. He could have gone on a Class III or IV but not Lava Canyon," replied Bechdel.

Bechdel's answer seemed to raise an incongruity.

Swindal probed the incongruity. "Mr. Bechdel, that raises an interesting question. I have read some of your promotional literature, and I saw where it said, 'No experience required'?"

"That is right," said Bechdel.

"And why is that?"

"Because my river is a whole lot easier and safer than the Chilko River."

Bechdel's testimony only got sharper edged as it progressed. There was Swindal's line of questions about Wolfe "coercing" Ron Thompson into taking only one raft and the failure to inform Jim Fasules of the dangers.

"What else is it about Needham's conduct that you believe was wrong in this case?" asked Swindal.

"Well, it became apparent to me, reading the literature provided to me, that Mr. Wolfe put a lot of pressure on Mr. Thompson to make it an exclusive trip. Wolfe didn't want any strangers on that trip, which caused Thompson to run a single-raft trip."

"But isn't that Thompson's problem? I mean, shouldn't Thompson have insisted that he go in two rafts?" asked Swindal.

"Yes, he should have," said Bechdel.

"But what if he didn't? Shouldn't Mr. Wolfe not have reassured him to run . . . ?"

"That's right, he shouldn't have."

"It is wrong, both ways you look at it?" inquired Swindal.

"Thompson messed up by running a single-raft trip, and I believe the reason he went on a single-raft trip was because Wolfe wanted the exclusivity. Wolfe didn't want anybody else to go on the river with them."

"Mr. Bechdel, prior to 1987, did you ever talk anywhere in any of your literature about not giving into pressure?"

"Well, yes. We talk about leadership. In my classes, I talk about the need to be forceful and sometimes say no. That is a necessary thing, even though it might displease some people. If you are going to compromise safety, there is a time you have to say no."

"Now, Mr. Bechdel, what else is there about Needham's conduct that you think was improper in this case?"

"Well, they didn't warn Mr. Fasules at all. I mean, it was merely a phone invitation."

The day was running long, and the judge was becoming impatient with the young plaintiff's attorney, Phillip Goldberg. From the trial transcript:

MR. GOLDBERG: Judge, we are almost at 5:00 o'clock. Clearly I am going to have a little bit more with Mr. Bechdel.

THE COURT: How much longer do you have? Better than an hour ago you told me 45 minutes.

MR. CROWE: That is lawyer's time, Judge.

THE COURT: I know that. How much longer?

MR. GOLDBERG: Believe me I would love to have gotten done an hour ago.

THE COURT: How much longer?

[*The judge persisted, tersely.*]

THE COURT: Let me give you some guidance. You repeat. You have asked one question about three or four times. He gives an answer and you repeat it two or three times. So we could probably shorten this up a few minutes, if we curtail the repetition. Secondly, the witness can testify about the nature and extent of safety warnings and those other kinds of things. Where you are starting to bump into problems is him passing judgment on whether it is negligent for someone to not have done something out of the area of expertise. In other words, there may well be a relationship that governs who is supposed to do what or what have you. He has testified what is typical about people who arrange the trip, and I allowed that testimony because I think that is okay. But for him to give opinions about negligence in certain instances on Needham's part beyond his expertise is inappropriate. I don't remember the question that I sustained the objection to, but it had to do with legal liability, if you will, on a situation, I think, between Needham and Thompson and it is something beyond his capacity to testify to. So that is where the problem is.

MR. GOLDBERG: It is youthful exuberance, Judge.

[*The cross-examination then continued. Goldberg was apparently rolling his eyes during the cross-examination, and the judge had had enough.*]

THE COURT: Let me interrupt you and see counsel at sidebar.

THE COURT: Mr. Goldberg, you are a young man and you are try-ing a good case, but to make facial gestures and reactions when I rule adversely to you, I will not tolerate that.

MR. GOLDBERG: Yes, Judge.

THE COURT: If you want to make an objection, make an objection. If I rule adversely to you, then sit there and take it like a professional.

MR. GOLDBERG: I didn't mean to, Judge.

Swindal continued with his cross-examination of Bechdel in an exchange that must have proved a little embarrassing when it pointed outed inconsistencies in Bechdel's own business procedures.

"Mr. Bechdel, directing your attention to Plaintiff's Exhibit 76, which is your older brochure, is it not?"

"That's correct," responded Bechdel.

"On the picture of that brochure there are several people in a raft, correct?"

"That's right."

"Is that one of your rafts?" Swindal asked.

"That's right."

"How many of them have helmets on?" asked Swindal.

"None of the people have helmets on," admitted Bechdel.

"Sir, in Exhibit 77, as I open it up to the flyleaf, there is a bigger picture of people in a raft, correct?"

"That's right."

"Is that, again, one of your rafts?"

"Yes," confirmed Bechdel.

"How many of them have helmets on?"

"Not one."

And then there was an interesting line of questioning about Ron Thompson's stellar safety record. Swindal asked the question he already knew the answer to: "You are not aware of any accidents on the Chilko River involving Ron Thompson prior to this one, are you?"

"I don't think I found out anything about any other accident," replied Bechdel.

"In fact, Mr. Bechdel, you didn't find out about any other accidents, period, on the Chilko River prior to August 1, 1987, did you?"

"No, I didn't find any at all."

"And, in fact, Mr. Bechdel, you would expect that a mature, sophisticated adult would know that these are the risks before embarking on a whitewater trip, wouldn't you?"

"Yes. I think every adult would know . . . ."

"Sir, your answer was 'yes.' You don't need to expound further," stated Swindal.

"What—what's the question about, drowning in water? Yes, every adult knows you can drown in water," Bechdel replied flippantly.

"Right. And even more so, Mr. Bechdel, you would assume that a sophisticated businessman and a former retired senior executive of a large corporation would understand and know that risk, wouldn't he?"

"To drown in water, yeah."

"We're not talking about a bathtub, as you did in your answer, Mr. Bechdel. I'm talking about whitewater rafting," said Swindal.

Bechdel had started to play word games, and Judge Kocoras dressed him down for it: "Limit the comments to the question put, Mr. Witness. Just answer the question put. We don't need this byplay. Go ahead. Put the question again."

Swindal said, "Thank you, your Honor.

Swindal resumed his questioning. "Mr. Bechdel, you would assume, would you not, that a sophisticated businessman and a former retired senior vice president of a large corporation would understand and know that he could drown while whitewater rafting?"

"Yes."

"And if he didn't know enough about whitewater rafting, this sophisticated senior executive vice president would know to ask, wouldn't he? Yes or no, Mr. Bechdel?"

"No."

"He wouldn't know to ask?" asked Swindal.

"What, if you can drown?" replied Bechdel

Swindal persisted with the question. "If he was concerned about it at all, he would know to ask, would he not? Yes or no?"

"It's tough to give a yes or no answer," said Bechdel.

"Mr. Bechdel, the ultimate decision to go whitewater rafting, when it comes right down to it, belongs to the individual participant, isn't that right?"

"That's right."

"Mr. Bechdel, James Fasules knew that he could drown if fell out of the raft in Lava Canyon on August 1, 1987, didn't he?"

"He knew he could drown if he fell out of the raft, yes," replied Bechdel.

And finally, this riposte from Bill Swindal about plaintiff attorney Phillip Goldberg's redirect examination of Bechdel. From the trial transcript:

MR. SWINDAL: Judge, Mr. Goldberg seems to be doing the testifying.

THE COURT: That is true. You have got to ask non-leading questions about what you pointed out.

MR. GOLDBERG: I don't have to worry about any more leading questions. That's it, Judge.

And so concluded the rather tense and tortured testimony of the plaintiff's whitewater expert Les Bechdel.

# Chapter Ten

Debra Davy called the rafting outfitter Ron Thompson to the stand to testify for the defendant. Thompson, a Canadian citizen, was clearly outside the subpoena power of the court, so he voluntarily agreed to appear at the courthouse in Chicago to provide his side of the story.

Not surprisingly, the questioning immediately proceeded to his decision to take one raft on the river. Thompson was unequivocal that he—and he alone—made that decision. Davy asked him about the decision to keep the Needham group isolated.

"Did you ever talk with Mr. Wolfe about keeping his group exclusive?" asked Davy.

"Yes," replied Thompson.

"All right. Did you talk with him about that more than once, if you can recall?"

"No."

"Do you remember the conversation?"

"I don't remember the specific conversation, but I remember the circumstances of it."

"Could you please tell us?" asked Davy.

"It was on the morning of the first day of the trip. There was a lot of indecision among Al's group as to who was going to do Lava Canyon that day, and initially I had been told that there were only two people wanting to go. And so I talked to the people at the lodge, and they had some people who also wanted to go. So that made eight people altogether. And then as we were getting ready to go in the morning, it turned out that Al had six people that wanted to go. And rather than have them all in the same boat, that being a dozen, he wanted—he asked me if he could have his party of six separate from the other people, in their own boat, and we did that."

"So on that day, how many rafts were used?" asked Davy.

"Two."

"And how many people were in each one?"

"Six."

Davy then asked Thompson to describe the day of the accident.

"Now, on August 1, 1987, there was an accident on the Chilko River, is that correct?"

"Yes."

"You were the guide and the trip leader?"

"Yes," said Thompson.

"And how many persons were in the raft that was involved in the accident?"

"Al Wolfe's party of 11 plus myself."

"Twelve people?"

"Yes."

"Was a decision made by anybody as to how many rafts would be used that day for how many people?"

"Yes."

"Who made the decision?" asked Davy.

"I did," replied Thompson.

"Did anyone else influence your decision?"

"No. The decision was made because I have had a working relationship with Chilko Lake Wilderness Ranch, where they had stayed, and they had people who wanted to do Lava Canyon with us on the second day but were unable to because of the weather, and they all came down on that same day. And there were 12 people in that group."

"All right."

"So they went with John McAlpine in the boat ahead, and I took Al Wolfe's party," Thompson stated.

Davy asked Thompson if there was anything remiss on the day of the accident. "On the Saturday, the day of the tragedy, August 1, 1987, did you notice anything at all unusual about the river?"

"No."

"Did you notice anything unusual about the raft?

"No."

"Was there anything that you noticed unusual about the passengers that day?

"No," said Thompson.

"Prior to the raft trip on August 1, 1987, was there anything that you can recall that caused you concern prior to entering the Lava Canyon?"

"No."

"Prior to entering the Lava Canyon, did you think there was anything dangerous about that boat trip?"

"Not particularly," Thompson replied.

"Prior to this accident, have you ever had a life-threatening experience or a capsize on the Chilko River?" asked Davy.

"No."

"Do you know anyone who had?"

"I have known of a capsize."

"Do you know as we sit here today whether there were any deaths prior to this occurrence on the Chilko River?"

"Not that I'm aware of."

Davy asked Thompson to describe the events leading to the horrendous accident in White Mile.

"Would I be correct that the raft struck a rock in Lava Canyon?"

"Well, I don't necessarily agree with that," said Thompson.

"Okay."

"What happened?" asked Davy.

"Well, the raft came up against a rock, and there is a cushion of water that's between the slow water in front of the rock. As the water approaches an object, there's a cushion around it, and the boat came up onto that cushion, and rather than striking the rock itself, that cushion lifted the boat, and the boat was pushed by the upstream water up onto its edge. Whether or not it actually contacted the rock may be incidental, but I don't know that."

Davy asked, "Do you know what caused you to come in contact with that cushion of water or with the rock?"

"I can't say that I know, but my idea would be that the large waves immediately above that pushed us over that way, and then the currents present at the time continued pushing us that direction."

"Had this ever happened to you before?"

"No," said Thompson.

Thompson expounded on the next series of events, particularly his rescue of Jim Fasules, who apparently had gotten *back* into the river after Thompson took him to shore—an astounding revelation that changed the complexion of everything. Naturally, this testimony would later be ridiculed by the plaintiff's lawyer in his closing argument since that rescue would decimate his case if Fasules had voluntarily subjected himself to the river after being allowed to escape it.

"What happened next after the encounter with the cushion of water or the rock?"

"Well, I was immediately thrown into the river, and I pretty much assumed at the time that the boat had flipped over. And I couldn't see anybody or anything for the immediate time afterwards. There were a few waves that I went through that went over my head. And then I was near the center of the river and drifted toward the left, and I remember kind of focusing on two holes—not big holes, but when you're in water up to your neck, they did look pretty big—that I went through, and then it was relatively flat below that, and I was floating toward the left-hand shore at that time. So I looked over toward the left-hand shore, and Jim Fasules was floating along near the shore, and so I swam over immediately below him while he was floating along on his back and . . ."

"What happened next?" asked Davy.

"We made eye contact and everything. I swam kind of around in front of him, and it was about waist- to chest-deep water there. I tried to stand up and kind of took a few steps downstream with the current and grabbed his arm and just kind of swung him into shore."

"What happened next?"

"We were stopped at shore. I asked him if he was okay, and he smiled and nodded. I told him to just stay right there. At that point I noticed that the boat was still coming behind us and that it was still upright with the oars in it."

"Let me stop you here for a moment, if I may. How close was Mr. Fasules to the shore at the point that you are talking about now?"

"Well, he was sitting probably in water up to his waist, but he was sitting stationary on the side of the river," replied Thompson.

"Did it appear to you that he understood you and was aware?"

"It appeared that he did. When I first saw him, he did not appear to be panicking in any way. Even when I grabbed a hold of him, he kind of grabbed my wrist at the same time. It was not like approaching a panicking drowning victim or something."

Davy then asked Thompson about the next sequence of events when Thompson saw Jack Collins inside the boat and Earl Madsen and Art Zeikel hanging onto it.

"Okay. So, I think you were just saying you turned around and you saw the boat. Is that right?"

"Yes," said Thompson.

"What happened next?"

"Well, Jack Collins was in the boat, and Earl Madsen was in the water holding onto one end of it. Art Zeikel was holding onto the other end of the boat. It kind of drifted toward the same shore that I was on. When I saw it coming in, I started scrambling upriver as fast as I could to get up near to it. I wanted to get close to it while it was still in the edge of this eddy."

"Why?"

"Well, I wanted to get back into the boat because I felt that that would be the best place for me to be of help to everyone," replied Thompson.

"Were you able to get back into the boat?"

"No, I wasn't. Before I got up there, Art Zeikel let go of the boat and just swam into shore. It was very calm right there. It was like swimming in a swimming pool. The boat just kind of caught the current and headed out into the middle of the river."

"Were you able to have any conversation at all with either Mr. Collins or Mr. Madsen in and holding onto the boat?"

"Well, Jack Collins was in the boat, and he was very indecisive about what to do. He was kind of turning one way and then the other way, and I just yelled at him to row the boat."

"Do you know whether he heard you and responded?

"Yes, he did. It was obvious that he did. He got in the center and grabbed a hold of the oars."

Thompson continued with his description of what transpired next. "I went up to Art Zeikel and instructed him to proceed down along that shore of the river, and I wanted to get up to the rock. There was water flowing around the rock between it and the shore, and I wasn't certain what had happened, but I knew at that point that I wasn't much help to anyone down the river and wanted to make sure that no one was still upriver where the accident had occurred."

"Let me stop you here. When you say you went up to the rock, are you talking about the rock that the raft either came in contact with or climbed up?"

"Yes," said Thompson.

"Now, when you say that you instructed Art, are you talking about Mr. Zeikel?"

"Yes."

"And, to the best of your memory, what did you tell him?"

"Just to go follow that edge of the river along and gather up anyone who might be there because at the same time that I was pulling Mr. Fasules to shore, there was somebody else down the river ahead of us who was floating along very close to the left-hand shore."

"Do you know who it was?"

"I don't know. At the time I assumed that it was Gene Yovetich."

Thompson told of leaving the river to get help as the disaster was quickly unfolding before his eyes.

Davy asked, "What happened next after you spoke to Mr. Zeikel?"

"I just went on up to the rock. At that point I wanted to get up to the road as quickly as possible because there was a reasonable chance that the vehicles had not yet gone past that point."

"What vehicles are you referring to?" asked Davy.

"The two vans that we had along on this trip."

"How long did it take you to get up to the road?"

"Not very long. It's kind of a gravelly bank that comes down to the river, and the road at that point is within 100 yards of the river."

"Please continue. What happened next?" instructed Davy.

"Well, I got to the road and then followed the road toward our destination point for the day."

"Did you see up until this point any other of the men that had been in the accident other than the ones that you have already told us about?"

"Well, when I was climbing up the bank, I could see Mike Miles and Jim Morrison on the far side of the river," said Thompson.

"Did you have any contact with them?"

"We did a little yelling back and forth, but I couldn't hear what they were saying, and I don't imagine they could have hear what I was saying either."

Thompson said he ran down the road about 11 miles and reached the point where the vehicles were waiting at the Taseko junction.

Davy asked, "What, if anything, did you do after that?"

"Well, I sent some private people in a car down the road 10 miles to the nearest house to call for help. And I had John McAlpine and the others go and get another raft and load it up on top of the van. As soon as they were loaded up, I put the boat in the river and rode the boat down."

Davy asked Thompson to describe how he then rescued Mike Miles, Joe Morrison, and Art Wolfe.

"Well, I took the boat down the river all by myself with no one in it until I found Mike Miles and Joe Morrison on the shore. And then we proceeded until we found Al Wolfe and picked him up. And he told us that there had been some kayakers that had stopped, and they said they had also found someone else—which I believed at the time was Bob Goldstein—and that he had no pulse or anything. And they kind of secured his body and marked it somehow. But we hadn't seen it floating by. I guess I need to backtrack a little bit, too. On the road we met a van, and they stopped, and Art Zeikel was in that van. And he got out and told me that he hadn't found anybody along that side of the river. And that was really the first time that I feared for the worst because I felt there should have been one, and most likely two, people on that side not very far downstream. So we floated down to the Taseko junction."

Davy asked Thompson about the strange occurrence of Jim Fasules appearing back in the river after Thompson had rescued him and brought him to shore, indicating that perhaps Fasules had jumped back into the river, perhaps to catch up with the others. If such a development were true, it would show that Fasules had been rescued, acted recklessly, and was responsible for his own death.

"Well, could you tell us how Mr. Fasules caught up with that raft?"

"I couldn't tell you because I didn't witness the whole thing. Objects—particularly in water like that—move at all kinds of different speeds. The raft was not under any kind of control, so it's very difficult to say what happened."

"But the raft swept past you in the current, isn't that right?" Davy asked.

"Yes."

"Do you figure Mr. Fasules dove in the water and swam after it, sir?"

"The point at which the raft swept past me was some distance upriver from where I had left Mr. Fasules," responded Thompson.

"Fasules was already on the shore now, and the raft sweeps by you, isn't that right?"

"Yes."

"Do you think Mr. Fasules could have dove in and swam and caught the raft by swimming?"

"I doubt very much that he dove," said Thompson.

"Do you think maybe he jogged along the riverbank and caught up with it and then dove in?"

"No, but however he ended up back into the river, he may have been back in the river before the raft went by me," replied Thompson.

Davy seemed confused. "Because when you took him, you didn't put him on the shore. You brought him to a point where he was only waist-deep?"

"Yes," said Thompson.

"The man at least that you think was Fasules?"

"I knew who Jim Fasules was," Thompson said.

"You knew, sir?"

"Yes," said Thompson.

"You knew Jim Fasules to be probably one of the quieter men on that trip, wasn't he, sir?"

"Yes, he was."

"And he was very, very gentlemanly, wasn't he?"

"Yes, he was."

Thompson was then dismissed as a witness and left the courtroom, but he later told reporters, "This time the wave hit us very hard and dumped a lot of water into the boat. It has always been a tricky passage. Half the time it pushes you to the left but most of the time not hard enough to get above that rock. There's normally a cushion of water that helps you ferry past. You rarely contact the rock, maybe 10 percent of the time.

"This time, we hit a slow, sluggish patch of water that brought the boat sideways. Then the wave drove us hard into the side of the rock. The upper part of the boat—away from the rock—was forced down. The other side stood on its side. People on the high side fell out. Those on the low side washed out. I was in the middle, steering with the oars, and I must have been one of the first out."

Thompson continued. "It's pretty disorienting when you hit the water. You go through the same wave, then try to recover a bit and get your wits about you. But in this place, you don't have that opportunity."

Thompson explained that the river moves at such velocity that those who are carried away may not be able to surface. "I didn't swim the whole thing," Thompson said. "It put me into an eddy of slower water on the left about 100 yards below the wave, where I was able to reach shore. Three other people [Michael Miles, Joe Morrison, and Art Zeikel] were across the river and okay. The rest [Jim Fasules, Bob Goldstein, Stu Sharpe, Al Wolfe, and Gene Yovetich] were downstream."

Thompson concluded, "There are probably tougher rafting rivers in Canada. I would guess the thing about Lava Canyon is not its toughness but its length. Because of the tremendous forces through those rocks, it has been recognized that if anything happened there, the results would not be good. There are those who believed that it was only a matter of time before something would happen."

# Chapter Eleven

To prove their case that Jim Thompson had followed all of the government regulations required of whitewater rafting outfitters, the defendant presented its expert witness, Dan Culver, who happened to be one of the first boaters to ever run the Chilko River.

Culver was a very experienced paddler, and he had served as an expert witness for the coroner's inquest for a joint inquiry into the deaths on the Chilko in 1987. This was a prestigious position that required him to closely review the documents that were collected by the Royal Canadian Mounted Police and provided to the coroner as well as to prepare the report of inquiry that was issued at the end of the inquest.

Dan Culver had also served as an expert witness for the coroner's inquest in 1979 looking into rafting deaths on the Fraser River. He was then retained by the Canadian government to help set standards for rafting in the provinces, and in 1981, the Province of British Columbia issued written standards for whitewater rafting.

At the time of trial, Culver was the chairman of the River Outfitters Association of British Columbia. During his impressive career on the river, Culver had worked as a professional rafting guide on the Thompson, Fraser, Chilko, and many other rivers, so he was eminently qualified to serve as defendant's expert.

Culver began his testimony by pointing out that prior to the deaths on the Fraser in 1979, there had been no rafting fatalities in British Columbia and that between the deaths on the Fraser and the deaths on the Chilko in 1987, there had been no drownings—"a remarkable safety record," Culver asserted, especially considering that "there had been thousands of trips run during that period." In 1981, the British

Columbian government issued its comprehensive "Standards and Conditions" for river outfitters in the province.

Davy first asked Culver about the requirement for two rafts on a trip.

"Is there anything within the written standards requiring on any river in British Columbia two rafts?"

Culver replied, "There was a very particular reference made at that time on the Fraser River, which was considered one of the very dangerous rivers in the province, and that under specific circumstances you were required to have two rafts in that river and that the rest of the time a one-raft trip was fine."

"Under what specific circumstances, sir, would you have to use two rafts on the Fraser River?" asked Davy.

"The standards say, 'At least two inflatable rafts shall be used when the water temperature is below 11 degrees Celsius or the cubic-feet-per-second reading is between 150,000 and 175,000 cubic feet per second.'"

"Can you translate 11 degrees Celsius into Fahrenheit?" asked Davy.

"I am Canadian, so I should be able to. Let's see, that would be about 52 degrees Fahrenheit."

"Do you recall, as we sit here today, what the temperature was on the Chilko River on the accident in this case?"

"I have read that it was 59 degrees," replied Culver.

Davy asked the obvious question. "Was there at that time any requirements for two rafts on Chilko if it was 59 degrees?"

"There was no requirement for two rafts in the Chilko," replied Culver

Davy then asked Culver about the overloading of rafts. "Now, did these government standards speak at the time—and again I am referring to written government standards, not the industry standard of care that rafting companies did on their own—was there a government requirement about how many people you could carry on a single raft at a single time?"

"Yes, there was."

"Could you show us and tell us for the record where it is in standards, sir?"

"Yes, it says, 'The number of persons on board a raft shall not exceed the number determined using the following formula.' And there is a formula which uses the maximum number of persons and the maximum weight capacity in kilograms."

"Do you recall, when looking at the standard for the coroner's inquest, if this formula was used in analyzing the capacity and the persons on Ron's boat?"

"I do recall that," said Culver.

"What was the result of that application of this formula to the number of people that went with Ron Thompson in August 1987 on the Chilko River?"

"The capacity for the boat in Ron's case was 16.59 people," Culver replied.

"Do you recall whether or not the inquest determined the appropriateness or overloading of Ron's raft?" asked Davy.

"They said it was not overloaded."

Davy next asked Culver about the use of life jackets. "Do the written standards at the time speak to the use of life jackets?"

"Yes, it does. It requires the approval standards of life jackets meeting the buoyancy and material requirements for each person on board."

"Okay. And do you recall from your investigation into the event of this case whether or not Mr. Thompson had one approved jacket for each person?"

"Yes, he did," replied Culver.

"Do you recall whether each person was wearing one approved life jacket prior to the entry into the Lava Canyon?"

"From the evidence I have seen, yes."

"Was there anything in the documents that you looked at for the coroner's inquest and inquiry that spoke to whether or not the life jackets were checked prior to the entry into the Lava Canyon?"

"The evidence was that they were checked prior to the entry into the Lava Canyon. In fact, Ron changed his life jacket for one of the passengers where he felt that their life jacket perhaps wasn't up to the standard of his," replied Culver.

Davy's interrogation then went into the adequacy of the life jackets used by Thompson.

"Now, the standard here speaks to an approved life jacket. Do you know what types of life jacket were approved at the time?"

"I am well aware of it. I designed the life jacket that was approved, and the jacket that Ron used—and that we all used—was the only life jacket approved in Canada for commercial river rafting."

"When you say that you designed it, were you working for Ancient Mariner?"

"I wasn't working for them. I helped Ancient Mariner design the jacket," said Culver.

"Was this part of your function as the chairman of the ROABC [River Outfitters Association of British Columbia]?"

"And my interest in rafting safety," stated Culver.

"Now, this jacket did not have a crotch strap, right?"

"That is correct."

"Why not, if you know?"

"Well, at the time, we considered a crotch snap and felt that [the] possibility that you might get hung up on the crotch strap made it less than suitable for what we wanted."

Davy continued. "Do you know whether any other state, province, or country on August 1, 1987, mandated the use of jackets with crotch?"

"I only know of North America, and I don't know of any in the United States or Canada."

The testimony then turned to helmets. "Now, returning to the written standards that were in effect at the time, sir, was there a requirement about helmets?"

"No, there was not," said Culver.

"All right. Do you know whether, aside from the written requirements, any commercial rafters either in your organization or working in Canada regularly used helmets?"

"In particular, I can recall on a river near the coast, the Chilowac River, which is a very small river that was run by paddle rafts, helmets would be issued because with paddle rafts—I experienced this myself—there is a chance of getting hit in the head with other paddles from your partners in the raft."

Davy pressed the issue. "You just said that helmets were not required in British Columbia, and you told us of an instance where some were used. Do you know as we sit here today whether at the time of this accident there was a requirement or a practice or standard in any other country requiring helmets in whitewater rafting?"

"I don't know of any."

"You don't know of any or you just don't know?" asked Davy.

"I don't know of that. I can't think of an instance where that was a requirement."

Then Davy moved to the subject to wetsuits. "Now, let's talk about wetsuits. Did the written standards in effect at the time of this occurrence mandate the use of wetsuits at all?"

"No, they did not," said Culver.

Next was the topic of rescue ropes. "Did these standards or written government regulations at the time impose an obligation of any kind to use rope throwers on the side or other spotters on any rivers?"

"No, they did not."

"Do you know anyone who ran commercial whitewater trips in British Columbia who regularly used those?" asked Davy.

"No, I don't."

"Do you know as we sit here today whether at that time there were any standards or regulations in North America mandating the use of such?"

Culver responded, "I don't propose to be an expert on that, but I have reviewed regulations for various rivers in the States and Canada and I haven't come across that."

Davy next broached the subject of Ron Thompson's general compliance with the safety regulations given that when the accident occurred, Thompson did not possess a valid license to operate as a commercial rafting outfitter.

"Based upon your participation in the coroner's inquest into this accident, as well as your knowledge of the written regulations at the time, my question first is, Do you have an opinion, to a reasonable degree of river rafting safety certainty, whether or not Ron Thompson was in compliance with the written standards and conditions at the time of this occurrence?"

"I believe that at the time, he did not have a license, but other than that, he was in compliance with the written standards," answered Culver.

Thompson had been active in developing the government regulations that governed river outfitters, and Davy asked Culver about his participation in those efforts. "You mentioned that Ron Thompson was involved in some manner in helping put together the written standards and regulations that were in effect at the time. What do you remember about that his involvement?"

"Well, Ron, along with the rest of us, participated in a lot of meetings and discussions to determine what would be the safest way to operate raft trips in British Columbia. He was very much a part of those working groups."

"Other than the lack of a permit in 1987, did the inquest find that Ron Thompson was in violation of any other written government standard?" asked Davy.

"No, the inquest said that Ron complied with standards. In fact, he probably went above."

"Aside from the written standards and requirements, do you have an opinion, based upon your knowledge and experience in the industry at the time, whether Ron Thompson violated a standard of care that existed at the time outside of the written requirements?"

"No, Ron was considered to be the best at what he was doing on the Chilko River," replied Culver.

"From what you know from investigating this occurrence, was he in violation of any standard of care that exceeded or should have exceeded the government requirements?"

"No, he was not."

Then came a discussion of how the rapids on the Chilko were officially rated on the international whitewater scale ranging from Class I to Class VI.

Davy inquired of Culver, "In general, if you can recall, how was the river rated at the time by those of you in British Columbia, even if it wasn't written down by the government?"

"It was rated a Class IV."

Davy asked for further clarification. "What does that mean, please?"

"Class IV in a system goes from zero to six. And zero is a lake, and six is impossible to run without extreme risk to life. A Class IV would mean more than a decked canoe could run but a river that was probably unobstructed and could consistently be navigated in a safe manner. It is subjective. It is not a Class V. It is not extremely difficult."

"Was the Chilko consistently run in a safe manner prior to this accident?"

"Yes," said Culver.

"Okay. No other accidents prior?"

"No, it was consistently safely run."

"We have heard that there was an accident on this river several days or so after this one. Was this a rafting accident?" Davy inquired.

Culver responded, "That accident several days later involved a party of two people who had flipped their raft and brought it to shore. One of the people decided to swim across the river to get some equipment and drowned in the process."

"Was that a swimming death, then, and not a rafting accident?"

"I would say yes," answered Culver.

"Are those the only two occurrences where death was involved on this river?"

"Yes."

The stress of a two-week-long trial was beginning to show on the judge and the lawyers, and a brief altercation occurred between the court and defendant's counsel over the questioning of regulations already in evidence. From the trial transcript:

MS. DAVY: Your Honor, could we try and clear this issue up outside the presence of the jury?

(Whereupon the following further proceedings were had at sidebar, out of the hearing of the jury, to wit:)

THE COURT: Everybody keep their cool and we will get along much better.

MS. DAVY: Your Honor—

THE COURT: Just relax a second, will you? I am running this show here.

THE COURT: I do not know what that is. We have a document that is in evidence that is the 1981 regulations. Use it so that we do not spend 10 minutes screwing around with whether this is the same as what the regulations are. There is a document in evidence. The witness apparently does not accept that what you are showing him are the 1981 regulations. I do not see why we need to have that dispute about it since we have a document in evidence which are the 1981 records. And if you have an objection, just stand and state it very simply. You do not need to get into a dither about it. You are acting unprofessionally about it. Let's go.

MR. CROWE: Judge, can I ask him what it is, then?

THE COURT: No.

Brian Crowe then began his cross-examination of Dan Culver by asking about whether the "accepted safety standard" governing outfitters necessitated the use of two rafts. The exchange became a little terse.

"Sir, is it true that before August 1, 1987, it was known and accepted in the river rafting industry in British Colombia that a minimum of two rafts on any trip is an essential safety requirement?" asked Crowe.

"In fact, the practice in British Columbia prior to August 1, 1987, was a very large number of trips were run with one raft. So the accepted industry standard was one or more rafts," Culver replied.

"I am not asking you what was done. I am asking you what the acceptable industry standard was, sir."

"I just explained to you that the acceptable industry standard is set in British Columbia by what was done. And what was done was the acceptable industry standard, and it included many, many one-boat trips as well as trips with more than one boat."

Crowe stiffened. "So even if I am doing something wrong, once I do it, [it] becomes an acceptable standard of practice if I am a river guide. Is that correct, sir?"

"The suggestion you are making is that [it] is wrong, and I disagree with that," Culver replied curtly.

Obviously impatient with the exchange, Crowe went immediately to the crux of the issue. "My question is, Would it have been safer for Thompson to take two rafts?"

"Safer is a subjective term. I can't tell you it would have been safer," responded Culver.

"Let us suppose that the Thompson raft was the lead raft and there was a trailing raft, all right? If someone fell out of the Thompson raft like 11 of them did, wouldn't it be safer if there was a raft traveling 50 to 150 yards behind?"

Culver refused to bite. "I am sorry, but I can only deal with a safety situation relative to results."

"Wouldn't it be possible that people in the second raft could help people out who fell in the water from the first raft?"

"I think on the Chilko it is not very likely that they could," Culver said.

"And if that second raft came along, perhaps someone else could stick their hand out and help someone in the water, isn't that true, sir?"

"It is unlikely they would be near the bodies, but it is somewhat a possibility," Culver admitted.

"And if the body were caught on a strainer or a boulder, then the second raft could come by and help them, couldn't it, sir?"

"There are no strainers on the Chilko, and the body wouldn't get caught on boulders the way the river's hydraulics function."

By this point, Crowe was beginning to show his frustration at Culver's refusal to answer the questions the way Crowe had hoped. So Crowe attempted to impeach Culver by showing his inconsistent views on how the river's rapids were rated. Culver refused to take the bait.

"In 1972, you regarded the Chilko River as a Class V river, didn't you, sir?" asked Crowe.

"In '72, after I had run it once, I said that it was a Class IV with several Class V drops. The first time, everything seems larger. At that time, which was in the infancy of river running, it was perhaps regarded by some as Class V drops. Now it is regarded as a Class IV river."

Crowe was insistent on having Culver admit that two rafts are safer than one and that a safety kayaker is a virtual necessity. But Culver's answer was so full of qualifications that it was useless to the plaintiff.

"Sir, let's go back then to the two-raft situation. You told about someone falling out of the lead raft and people in the following raft not being able to help. Let's turn it around the other way. Let's suppose that it's people out of the back raft that fall into the water. Would the lead raft do any good?"

Culver admitted, "A lead raft could help sometimes in that situation."

"Could help rescue people in the water?"

"Could help," Culver said.

"If a safety kayak was following along, could that also be of some help?"

"Sometimes," conceded Culver

Failing with that line of questioning, Crowe wanted to show the inherent danger of rafting. But then he went too far, and Culver called him on it.

"Isn't it a fact that you think that people go rafting because they are risking their lives?"

"I wouldn't put it that way. I think people know when they go rafting that there is some risk. I think some of that excitement must be part of

them going. I wouldn't go as far as to say they know that they are risking their lives."

"Do you ever say to people, 'Do you know you might die on this trip?
You might fall in the river and drown?' Do you give them that instruction before you take them on a trip?"

"That's a pretty general question. I don't think that I would com-
monly say that."

"You don't tell them about drowning either, do you, sir?"

"I don't think that's generally what I would do."

Crowe wasn't about to give up, so he asked Culver about the adequacy of the safety instructions that Thompson gave to the rafting party
on the Chilko.

"Hypothetically, then, if no safety instructions were given, Mr.
Thompson would have deviated from acceptable standards of care,
wouldn't he, sir?"

"If none were given, but I understand that . . ."

Crowe persisted. "My question is a simple one. Would you answer
my question: If no instructions were given, would he have deviated
from acceptable standards of care?"

"Yes," replied Culver.

"If the only instructions that Thompson gave were to hold onto a rope
with one hand and hold onto a bar, he would have violated acceptable
standards of care, would he not?"

"There was a real variety in what was said as far as safety talks,"
replied Culver.

Crowe was now clearly annoyed. "Are you being an advocate here
today?"

Culver coyly responded, "What is an advocate?"

Crowe explained, "Someone who takes a position in a case and tries
to win it?"

"No," stated Culver.

Crowe continued. "Could you tell me the warnings that you would
give, sir, before you put someone in a raft?"

"I would discuss some of the items that are laid out in the standards,
such as wearing a life jacket, positioning in the raft, where to hang
on—things that I felt they needed to know [to] be comfortable in head-
ing down the river."

Crowe asked, "What would you tell them about if they fell in the water?"

"I would tell them to hang onto the side of the boat and, if separated from the boat, to swim for shore."

"Anything else?" asked Crowe.

"On some rivers—but not on that river—I would tell them to swim feet forward going down the river because of the chance of hitting rocks. But you could or could not tell them that on the Chilko because it was not significant to their safety. They're not likely to hit rocks."

"They are not likely to hit a rock on the Chilko River?" said Crowe.

"An individual is not likely to strike a rock on the Chilko," said Culver.

"So, it wouldn't matter what you told them about how they either swim like this [indicating] or on their back? It wouldn't matter on the Chilko, would it, sir?"

"My experience would be the best thing to do would be just to swim as best it works for you towards the shore," answered Culver.

"So, you would tell them, 'Do what's best for you in terms of swimming'?"

"On that river, yes. On small, rocky rivers, it would be very important to protect your head by having your feet first. On a river like the Chilko River, where you are not likely to hit rocks, it is quite deep, and it's a smooth channel of water with rapids, but it is an unobstructed channel. The best thing to do is just get to shore."

"Would you agree with this statement by Mr. McGinnis on the put-in talk: 'The put-in talk on a Class V river is a matter of life and death. Impress this fact on the trip members to motivate the group to listen with rapt attention. The trip leader might begin with something like this: 'This is an extremely dangerous river. Your chances of survival will be directly related to how well you listen to what I am about to say.' Would you agree with what McGinnis says about that?"

"Yes, even though the Chilko is a Class IV river, I think some strong statement would be appropriate," said Culver.

"Would you tell the people about going to the 'high side'?"

"Well, we usually told them, although it didn't usually make any difference."

"You would tell them about 'high siding' before they got in the raft, though, wouldn't you, sir?"

"Well, in this instance, I don't think you would know you were going to high side until you were there."

"So, no sense in practicing it, is that right, sir?"

Culver replied, "You can't practice a 'high side.'"

"You can't get in a raft and practice about all going to one side. You can't do that?"

"I suppose on flat water you could move across the raft to the other side, but that wouldn't significantly approximate high siding on a rock, where the raft is tipped up on the side."

With that unfruitful exchange behind them, Brian Crowe—who had done all he could to control his temper—gladly informed the court that he had no more questions for the frustratingly dexterous Dan Culver.

# Chapter Twelve

To prove that Ron Thompson had followed the established standards of the commercial whitewater rafting industry, Debra Davy called James Lavalley as an expert witness for the defendant.

Lavalley was exceptionally qualified to testify in this regard. He had been in charge of the examination process for British Columbia raft guides under the Ministry of Environment. He was also responsible for the grading of rivers and rapids run by rafting outfitters.

James Lavalley also worked for Rescue Three International of Sonora, California, teaching advanced swift-water rescue courses in Canada for professional river guides and search-and-rescue organizations. And from 1980 to 1989, he was the president and co-owner of Hyak River Expeditions in Vancouver, which operated commercial river trips in Alaska, Yukon, and British Columbia—including those on the Chilko River.

Debra Davy first sought to establish Ron Thompson's credentials through the testimony of James Lavalley. "How long did you guide trips down the Chilko River?" she asked.

"I began guiding on the Chilko River in 1974. I began guiding through Lava Canyon in 1980," said Lavalley.

"Other than you and Ron Thompson, were there any other outfitters who took people down the Lava Canyon?"

"Yes, there were a number of other outfitters—probably a total of 10. Thompson Guiding would have probably represented about 70 percent of the trips through Lava Canyon. My company, Hyak, would have probably represented about 20 percent, and the other eight companies would have represented the last 10 percent of people traveling through Lava Canyon."

"And when was the last time you traveled down the Lava Canyon of the Chilko River?"

"This past August—two trips."

"Now, when you operated down the Lava Canyon, did your group use more than one boat?" Davy asked.

"Yes, we did."

"What about Ron Thompson?"

Lavalley responded, "Ron Thompson specialized in single one-day trips, and I would imagine that 95 percent of his trips through Lava Canyon would be single-boat, single-day trips."

"Have you yourself ever run a single-boat trip with 11 people in the boat?"

"Yes, I have," answered Lavalley.

"On a Class IV river without helmets and wetsuits?"

"Yes."

"Where and when, sir?"

"The Thompson River in British Columbia."

"Did you ever have a position of leadership in the Rafting Outfitters Association of British Columbia?"

"Yes, I was the president from 1981 to 1982."

"And was that the same period of time during which the written government standards and regulations were drafted?"

"The regulations were drafted primarily in '79 and '80. I helped in the implementation."

"What was Ron Thompson's reputation as an outfitter?" asked Davy.

"Ron Thompson was looked upon as the expert on Lava Canyon and the Chilko River. He singularly rafted there. Ninety percent of his work would have been on that river. My company was the second-largest operating company on the Chilko through Lava Canyon, and we were small compared to that. Ron would have always been referred to as the expert on the Lava Canyon section of the Chilko River."

"Do you know whether he had a safety record on that river?"

Lavalley replied, "Yes, to my knowledge, there has never been a flipped boat or a prolonged swim on through the Lava Canyon section by anyone prior to August 1, 1987, including Ron."

"Do you have an opinion as to whether or not it was a violation from known standards of care or from the standards and regulations enforced at the time for Ron Thompson to have used only one craft on this trip?"

"No, it was not."

In her questioning, Davy then proceeded to clear Al Wolfe from any responsibility for the accident.

"Are you aware, due to your experience in the field, of the differences between the roles of a trip leader and guide—such as Ron Thompson—and a trip organizer—such as Al Wolfe—and a passenger—such as Mr. Fasules?"

"Yes," replied Lavalley.

"Are you aware of the different responsibilities and roles of the trip leader or guide, the trip organizer and the passenger?" asked Davy.

"Yes, I am very aware," said Lavalley.

"From all of the materials that you looked at in forming your opinions in this case, whose responsibility is it to manage safety and rescue operations on a trip such as this?"

"The trip leader," Lavalley firmly stated.

"Is it the responsibility or duty or role of an organizer of a trip to warn about safety hazards or risks or to train people how to rescue others in the water?"

"No, it is not."

"Is it the responsibility of a trip organizer to teach others how to save fellow passengers in the water?"

"No, it is not."

Davy persisted. "My question to you, sir, is, Did Al Wolfe do anything wrong that caused or contributed to Jim Fasules's death?"

"No," replied Lavalley.

"From what you have seen in the records, did Al Wolfe take any steps to ascertain Ron Thompson's competence or ability before he organized a trip in 1987 to the Chilko River?"

"Yes, he did," replied Lavalley. "Based on the experience I have dealing with group organizers over the last 18 years, the responsibility of a trip organizer is primarily to organize the group and to choose the operator. After reading the work that Mr. Wolfe did in choosing the outfitter, I personally have never had a group organizer do that degree of research before choosing an outfitter."

Davy then asked Lavalley to testify about Thompson's safety precautions. The exchange was fast-paced, piercing, and unequivocal.

"Do you have any opinions as to whether or not the safety precautions that Ron Thompson took affected or influenced or caused the death of Jim Fasules?

"Yes, I do."

"Did they?"

"No, they did not," stated Lavalley.

"So, the safety precautions were the first step in Ron's informing the individuals of what to do. What happened next that relates to your opinion that what Ron did not cause this accident? What else did he do?"

"Well, his safety talk on the land and then when they got in water, he showed them where to sit and how to hold on. And, again, at the top of Bidwell, he went over the major and important parts to the safety talk, specifically, the life jackets and how to swim in cold water," said Lavalley.

"Was that appropriate?" asked Davy.

"Yes, it was."

"Have you read the statement of Ron Thompson or the deposition of Ron Thompson as it specifically relates to anything he talked about with safety?"

"Yes, I have."

"And did the things that he talks about in his deposition and statement appear to be appropriate to you?"

"Yes, they are typically of safety talks on the river in and during that time," answered Lavalley.

"Is that the conclusion drawn in the coroner's inquest as well?"

"Yes, it is."

"What next did Ron Thompson do, if anything, that supports your opinion?"

"Well, continuing through Bidwell Rapids, I believe Thompson reemphasized that people should hold on. With people in front of him, a couple of the passengers had to lean back a little bit, and Thompson reemphasized that they should hold on and make sure they stay in that position."

"Was that appropriate?" Davy asked.

"Yes, it was if people are having trouble holding on."

Davy asked, "Do you know whether or not each individual was wearing a safety jacket that was approved and correctly done up at the time they entered the Lava Canyon?"

"Yes, from all of the evidence I have read, they were all using the Canadian Coast Guard approved high-float whitewater life jacket."

"Was there any evidence that Ron checked those jackets to make sure that they were secure before entering the Lava Canyon?"

"Yes, from evidence of the survivors, a check was done before Bidwell, and normally that is where it is done."

"That was appropriate?"

"Yes," said Lavalley.

"What next did he do that contributes to your opinion that Thompson didn't cause the occurrence in terms of safety precautions."

"Until the incident happened, I think he had covered all of the basic standard safety precautions, which is self-rescue, how the boat operates, how to swim in the river, how to pull people back in the boat. They were all basically covered before he went down the river."

"Did Thompson have within the 18-foot raft a throw bag or rope?" asked Davy.

"Yes, he had a throw bag, which was connected to the rowing frame, which is normal, and he had a floating bow and stern line, which is normal in an oar-powered boat."

"And that is appropriate?"

"Yes, and he also had perimeter lines around the boat, which is regulation."

Davy continued. "I would like to ask you about the safety precautions Ron took once the raft hit the rock that contributed to your opinion. We now have the raft hitting the rock, and he says, 'Get to the high side.' What else happened in terms of his behavior and safety precautions?"

"Well, after commanding the people to move to the high side, the evidence seems to indicate that he grabbed the throw bag, and at that time the boat broached fairly steeply. The guide is often in the least secure position because his hands are not, you know, holding onto anything solid. Thompson fell off the raft with the throw bag in his hand and down the low side and around the rock."

"And what next did he do after he fell out of the raft in terms of helping anybody or safety precautions or rescue techniques?" Davy asked.

"Well, when the raft broached, the people in the front of the boat would have gone into the river and down under the rock. Ron would have been with that initial group. At that time, the evidence seems to indicate that Ron surfaced in a comparatively quiet back eddy around 200 meters below. It seems that he had lost the throw bag during that time, which would be natural because he would be disoriented and upside down under the water."

Davy had Lavalley continue with his analysis of the accident.

"When he surfaced, what did he do, if anything, next in terms of helping anybody?"

"Well, there were a couple of things that happened fairly quickly. He told the people there to hold on. He then saw Jim Fasules in the eddy fairly close to him. He then approached and made a contact rescue of Mr. Fasules and towed him to the bank. He then motioned to, I believe, Mr. Collins, who was in the boat, to grab the oars and move the boat to shore."

"Does the evidence show that he yelled at Mr. Collins?"

"He yelled to Mr. Collins to grab the oars and move the boat to shore," said Lavalley.

"Does the evidence show anything about whether Mr. Collins was able to do that or heard it?"

"I don't know. Obviously not because Mr. Collins either didn't hear it or could not do that."

"What next?" asked Davy.

"With Mr. Fasules on the bank, Thompson then asked him if he was okay, and apparently he nodded and smiled, which would—from a rescue point of view—release Thompson, once he made contact with a victim, to go on and rescue other members of the group."

"And what happened next?"

"The evidence indicates he headed upstream to the rock, where the boat broached, being concerned that there would be someone entrapped in there. At that time, he came across Mr. Zeikel, I believe."

Davy asked, "What happened then?"

"Thompson instructed Mr. Zeikel to head down along the riverbank and collect anyone that may be there and keep moving down the river and assist anyone that made it to shore."

"Up to this point, are the actions that he took appropriate?"

"Yes, they are completely appropriate," relied Lavalley.

"What happened next?"

"I think at that time, the boat had moved down the river. Thompson had to make a decision to swim for the boat, and he decided not to. And at that time, I believe he noticed, I believe it was, Mr. Miles and Mr. Morrison on the other bank."

"Could he make any contact with those individuals, if you know?" queried Davy.

"Yes. Thompson yelled across to them and told Mr. Miles and Mr. Morrison to continue down the river right bank, to look for the boat and look for anyone else that may come to shore there."

"Were those actions appropriate?"

"Yes, that is appropriate river-rescue organization and delegation and after assessing the situation, trying to work your way down through the river system," reassured Lavalley.

"All right. What happened next?"

"After he assumed Mr. Zeikel had moved down the river left and Mr. Morrison and Mr. Miles were moving down the river right, Thompson then ran up the bank and tried to catch the van."

"Was he able to catch the van?"

"No, he was not," said Lavalley.

"What happened next?"

"He then ran down to the Taseko junction, and the evidence indicates that he then sent the driver to the nearest telephone to contact the Royal Canadian Mounted Police."

"All right. What happened next?"

"The police were contacted, another boat was brought up from Thompson's headquarters, and the boat was then put in the water."

"Now, are these events that you have just related to us and reflected in the Royal Canadian Mounted Police documents at the time?"

"Yes, I believe they are."

Davy began to sum up.

"Based upon your experience and training of individuals in swift-water rescue, were the actions taken by Mr. Thompson at the time of this accident, and specifically with respect to Mr. Fasules, appropriate lifesaving and rescue behaviors?"

"Yes, they are appropriate," said Lavalley. "The initial rule in rescue river rescue is self-rescue, which Mr. Thompson did and a number of the other clients did. The next thing he did directly was to make a contact rescue with Mr. Fasules, and in the scale of danger to a rescuer, contact rescue is one of the most dangerous. And in swift-water rescue where a fatality occurs, 50 percent of the fatalities are indeed rescuers."

"Fifty percent of the people who rescue other people die?" asked Davy, somewhat surprised.

"Fifty percent of the fatalities in swift-water rescue incidents are the rescuer."

In her questioning of James Lavalley, Debra Davy then went into the inevitable subject of one-boat trips.

"Based upon your knowledge and experience and the materials that you have reviewed in this case, do you have an opinion as to whether another raft on the river would have been able to help save Mr. Fasules?"

"I believe it would have not. It would have made no difference," replied Lavalley.

"Tell us why, please."

"Well, first of all, if Mr. Thompson had been running a multiple-boat trip, he would have been running the first raft."

"Why?" asked Davy.

"Thompson is the most experienced person, and the most proficient guide would always run the first raft because if the first raft does get into a problem—whether it's a one-boat, a two-boat, three-boat, or four-boat trip—he is generally on his own. Now, in continuous rapids, this is specifically the case. With oar-powered boats, you do not have forward speed on the water. So if an accident does happen in the first boat, in a comparatively long rapid—the White Mile is a little over a half a mile long—the second boat would not be able to apply speed to catch anyone in the main current. The second boat in a pool-and-drop type of river may be able to help at the end of the rapid. And in this situation Mr. Fasules would have been at the shore by the time the second boat would have gone by."

"What do you mean—that he would have been onshore?" asked Davy.

"Well, I think he would have been in an eddy. He would not have been in the mainstream."

"Why do you say that?"

"Well, the second boat would be trying to follow fairly close. In a multiple-boat trip in a rapid like the White Mile in Lava Canyon, it is very hard for two boats or three boats to stay in very close proximity to each other."

Davy continued. "Have you seen the video that was taken almost immediately after this occurrence, where Ron Thompson was in the helicopter with the Royal Canadian Mounted Police and they were filming over the river?"

"Yes, I have."

"All right. Is there anything within that video—which was shown to the jury during opening statements—that points outs any of the principles that you're talking about with these two rafts?"

Lavalley responded, "Well, I think the video indicates that the river was semicontinuous, that the boat went down with very little difficulty and very little maneuvering required. The time taken to run the White Mile section, I believe, was about four and a half minutes."

"Okay. From the materials that you looked at—the Royal Canadian Mounted Police statements at the time and the notes of the Mounties at the time—do you know how quickly it was that Ron Thompson and Mr. Fasules were out on the shore?"

"From the evidence that I have read, it would be between two and three minutes," answered Lavalley.

To wrap up her direct examination of Lavalley, Debra Davy then covered the other possibilities that would have save Jim Fasules's life—safety kayak, wetsuit, and helmet. Lavalley replied that, sadly, none of these would have made a difference.

Davy asked, "Based upon your experience and what you have looked at, if there had been persons up on the side of the cliffs or slopes who had throw ropes, could they have effected a rescue more quickly than two minutes?"

"No," replied Lavalley.

"Could a kayak, in your opinion, that was traveling along in the eddies on the side, if that had occurred, have effected a rescue more quickly than two minutes?"

"No," said Lavalley.

"Do you, sir, advocate the use of wetsuits in general?"

"Yes, we do on certain rivers."

"At the time that this accident occurred, were wetsuits and helmets required on this river?"

"No, they were not."

"Had a wetsuit or a helmet been used—had Mr. Fasules been wearing one—in your opinion, based on what saw and your experience, your training, rescuing individuals as you have, would that have made any difference to Mr. Fasules?"

Lavalley simply stated, "No."

"Why not?"

"Well, Mr. Fasules was in the water after the rafting incident for probably about two minutes. During that time, he would have experienced respiratory gas reflex, which is an uncontrollable increase in your respiration rate. And regardless of whether you had a wetsuit or a helmet, that would have happened."

"All right. Would I be correct in saying that wetsuits are thought to protect against hypothermia and to give you some flotation?"

"Yes."

"Okay. Did hypothermia play a part in Mr. Fasules's death?"

"No."

"Hypothermia takes a lot longer than a few moments?"

"Yes, in Betty Pratt-Johnson's book, at 59 degrees Fahrenheit, it would take approximately two hours in the water to have marginal hypothermia start to affect the core of the body."

"Helmets can protect, theoretically, against head injuries, can't they?"

"Yes, they can."

"Did Mr. Fasules die of a head injury?"

"No, he did not."

"What does the coroner's report say was the cause of Mr. Fasules's death?"

"Rapid asphyxiation."

"From the materials that you saw, did Mr. Fasules perish as a result of being trapped underneath any logs or obstacles?"

"No, he did not."

Debra Davy made the point clear.

"From the materials that you saw, was there anything at all remarkable or unusual about the condition of the individuals that ultimately perished as they were seen in the water shortly after the occurrence?"

"Well, hypothermia was thought to be the problem, and it was a surprise to all of us to realize that these people seemed to be in distress very quickly and had, in fact, gone into the pre-drowning syndrome within two or three minutes."

"Okay. From the materials that you looked at, sir, was there any evidence that Al Wolfe was responsible for putting all these gentlemen into one raft?"

"No," said Lavalley.

"From any of the materials that you saw from the victims and survivors at the time and from the coroner's inquest, did anyone say that this raft was overloaded?"

"No."

"From the materials that you looked at contained within the judgment of inquiry and all of the statements that were provided to the coroner in this case, did you see anything within those statements that this raft was overloaded or overcrowded?"

"Not that I can remember," Lavalley responded.

"From the materials that you looked at, sir, was there any statement by anyone other than a paid expert witness such as yourself or Mr. Bechdel that indicated that Mr. Fasules was surprised about going whitewater rafting?"

"No, not to my knowledge at all."

"Do you know how many people or persons were in Mr. McAlpine's raft that left an hour or so before on that Saturday and went down the river?"

"I believe there were 13," said Lavalley.

"Is the Lava Canyon or the Chilko River a Class V?"

"No, it's a Class IV river. I don't know of anyone that classifies it as a Class V."

# Chapter Thirteen

All of the evidence relating to *Fasules v. D.D.B. Needham Worldwide, Inc.*, was now in, and the court moved to the final stage of trial before jury deliberations. After two weeks of vigorous courtroom battle, Brian Crowe delivered the long-anticipated closing argument for the plaintiff.

Crowe approached the jury box with the confidence of a trial lawyer who, having done this many times before, relished the opportunity.

"Good morning, ladies and gentlemen. First of all, I want to thank you for the time away from your families, your occupations, and the attention that have been given to us all during the course of the trial. As the judge said, this is our opportunity to give a closing argument. It's the opportunity for lawyers to analyze the evidence as though we were one of the triers of fact. And it's also our opportunity to briefly discuss the law as we believe His Honor Judge Kocoras will instruct about the burden of proof.

"Let's then look at the evidence and the law in this case to see what is more probably true than not. We have filed an action against Needham, and it is the law of this case that Jim Fasules is an invitee of Needham. You need not concern yourself about that. We have brought an action against Needham under three theories, which His Honor will submit to you in the jury instructions.

"The first theory against Needham arises out of the actions of Al Wolfe. The judge is going to instruct you that corporations can only act through their employees. Al Wolfe was their employee, and Needham is liable for the acts of Al Wolfe. What did Al Wolfe do that was negligent and for which Needham is responsible?

"First of all, he failed to warn Mr. Fasules about the dangers of the Chilko River and the possibility that he might receive serious injuries and death. What warnings did Mr. Wolfe give Mr. Fasules? We're dealing here now with an individual, Al Wolfe, who was an experienced whitewater rafter. He did four trips on the Selway River, a Class IV river. He did one on the Middle Fork of the Salmon River. He did one on the Chilko in 1985. And he organized and planned this entire Chilko trip. He knew the dangers of the river and the risks of injury and death.

"Did he send Jim Fasules anything? Nothing. He was a last-minute fill-in, he says. What did Al Wolfe tell Jim Fasules to warn him of risk of death and injury? First of all, Al Wolfe said, 'Well, you see, I had a five- to ten-minute phone call.' He said this several weeks ago to make you believe he told Jim everything he needed to know about the Chilko River. When he came back this week, he now said the phone call was two minutes long.

"What did Al Wolfe say on the phone call? I think it's a fair inference that all he ever said to Jim was, 'Go talk to Gene.' Did he say, 'The wildest and woolliest river?' No. That was Al Wolfe's standard line. He said he told every man he called that it was a wild and woolly river. But three times at his deposition, he said, 'My standard line was the best 45 minutes of whitewater.'

"Would he tell Fasules 'the best 45 minutes of whitewater?' Of course not because Fasules had never been whitewater rafting in his life. So what he told him was, 'Go talk to Gene.' Gene, of course, is now dead. And there is no evidence that Gene Yovetich ever whitewater rafted in his life.

"What did Jim Fasules say to his wife after he hangs up after that phone call of a minute and 10 seconds? He said, 'Lenore, I want to go fishing.' And she said, 'So go.'

"Right after was a call to his son Gary Fasules in Glen Ellyn, Illinois, and that phone call, according to the phone records, lasted 10 minutes. And in that lengthy phone conversation, he talked about fishing and not one single word about rafting. Add to that the fact that Jim had no experience at whitewater rafting. He had absolutely no idea when he left what he was getting into.

"Needham is liable because Wolfe knew the dangers of the Chilko, and he didn't warn Fasules as he should have. Secondly, Needham is responsible, and Wolfe is responsible as their agent because he negligently exercised control over Ron Thompson. On that Thursday, you will recall, Thompson wanted to do it right—he wanted to take two rafts down the Chilko River. It was at this point that Wolfe said, 'I told that last outfitter, Steve Curry, when I was on the Selway, and I'm telling you, that this group is going to stay exclusive. There is going to be no other group with us.'

"What did Mr. Wolfe say in his deposition? 'I was explicit about it,' he said. 'We worked 60- to 70-hour weeks, and we weren't going to mix with any other people. We weren't going to mix with any Germans or couples from California. We're going alone.' Al Wolfe called the shots, and Thompson obeyed. Thompson succumbed to pressure, and he shouldn't have. And sure enough, what happened? On Saturday, how many rafts were available? One raft.

"Thompson took that other group and sent them downriver at another time. So they went in a single raft, jeopardizing their lives, too. And the same thing happened on Thursday. Al Wolfe and Needham are unquestionably liable for the pressure they put on Ron Thompson.

"Was Thompson wrong to accept the pressure? Of course he was. Was Wolfe wrong to do it? Of course he was. And Wolfe came in here and denied that he ever put pressure on Ron Thompson. But we know through John McAlpine, Thompson's employee, about the pressure. And McAlpine—you saw him right here on videotape—told you twice that pressure was put on Thompson by Needham. Needham is clearly liable for the acts of Wolfe, but the liability of Needham does not end with Al Wolfe because he had a most negligent accomplice in Ron Thompson."

In his typically organized and concise manner, Crowe moved to his second theory of liability—that rafting on the Chilko was an *inherently* dangerous activity.

"His Honor Judge Kocoras is going to instruct you that the plaintiff's second theory is that if you decide that the Chilko River running through Lava Canyon is inherently dangerous, then Ron Thompson became the agent of Needham, and Needham is liable for the acts of Ron Thompson.

"Is the Chilko River inherently dangerous? You have heard the testimony. The expert witnesses for the defendant came in and tried to make it sound like it was the lagoon in Lincoln Park, but we know better than that. It has been described by witnesses as the most challenging and dangerous river in North America. And even the defendant's expert witness said it is a relentless river—full of rapid after rapid of Class IV and Class V whitewater.

"And what was in that river? There are holes—holes as deep as the raft itself. There are hydraulics—waterfalls that can pin a person so they can't get out. There are boulders and boulder sieves and uncut rocks and strainers and logs across it. And it is remote—canyon walls that rise 200 feet into the air. And you saw the body of poor Bob Goldstein being pulled out of that river by helicopter in a strainer. He was pulled straight up because that was the only way they were able to get him out.

"And the sound, Collins said, was like a freight train running through a tunnel. On August 1, 1987, it was 118 cubic meters of water per second running through it—the highest it had ever been since 1981. And even Thompson himself said the river was 40 percent higher than it usually was. There is no doubt that the Chilko River is inherently dangerous.

"And Ron Thompson, did he do anything wrong? Sure he did. First of all, Thompson himself failed to warn Fasules. How? Well, what literature did he give Fasules? He never gave Fasules anything before he left his home in Ennis, Montana. And Thompson never gave Wolfe anything to give Fasules or anyone else about the fact that that river was Class V or the fact that you might get injured or that you might die.

"Do other rafting outfitters do that? Sure they do. They tell you what kind of river you're running. They ask you if you ever been whitewater rafting before, if you can you swim, and the state of your health. If you read a form like that, you say, 'Wait a minute. Somebody just told me about a Class V river—something I've never heard of. They tell me that I can be injured or I can die. Why do they want to know if I can swim? Why do they want to know if I've ever been whitewater rafting before? And, my God, why do they want to know what the state of my health is? I think maybe I should think about it real good.'

"When else was Wolfe given an opportunity to warn Mr. Fasules? Saturday morning. What kind of warning did he give Jim Fasules before that raft was put in to start its slow descent for 90 minutes to the mouth? Collins said Wolfe didn't give him any. And a lot of other witnesses said they didn't get any.

"Earl Madsen said that he didn't get any warning until he was at the top of Bidwell Rapids. Morrison said he didn't hear a warning. Zeikel doesn't say anything about warnings in his statement. The only person that says he gave instructions and warnings about what was going to happen is Thompson.

"And what kind of warnings was he supposed to give? Bill McGinnis, in his book *The Class V Briefing*, the authority in this nation and in Canada on whitewater rafting, says, 'This is what you say to people who go whitewater rafting.' He says, 'You say to them, 'Listen up and listen real well now. You might die. What you are going through here in the next few minutes is a matter of life and death.' And then McGinnis goes on and tells them what they're getting involved in and the dangers of the river.

"Ron Thompson did absolutely none of that. The die had been cast on Thursday. He only brought one raft. All 12 people—200- and 225-pound men—piled into that raft. What happened to the children and the women and the four men that were in the other group? Thompson told McAlpine, 'Take them down at another time and another place just like you did on Thursday?' Why? Once again, he was going to obey Wolfe. That raft was overcrowded, and it was not maneuverable.

"What else did Mr. Thompson do wrong? He took a raft down the river without providing wetsuits. He took a raft down the river without providing helmets for the people. He took a raft down the river without providing spotters along the shore. And we'll talk about that in a moment. He took a raft down the river without telling the people about throw ropes. He didn't tell them about how to save themselves or each other. None of the things that he should have done did Thompson do. And Needham is liable for his acts because the Chilko River is inherently dangerous.

"What else? There was no safety kayak following them either. All the things that he could have done and didn't. Why? Because it was a little clubby group out there that is thinking only of economics more than the general public.

"Let's see what the result of all that conduct was. The men are in the raft. They're floating along for 90 minutes. The water is calm and passive. There is no warning to Jim Fasules about what he is going to be facing. He doesn't know what the Chilko River looks like at this point. And they finally get to Bidwell Rapids.

"Are Fasules and the others frightened at this point? Sure they are. Do they have a choice to leave at the end of Bidwell? Well, you heard the evidence that there was no staff at the pickup point. There was a point right after Bidwell and before you entered the White Kilometer where a van could pick you up, but there was none of that here. And before they had gotten to Bidwell, the only instructions that were given was, 'Hang on. Keep a hand on the rope. Keep a hand on the metal bar.' That was the only warning given these men. And as that raft went through Bidwell and started into White Kilometer, the fruits of the negligence of Wolfe and the fruits of the negligence of Thompson finally bore out."

With the jury on the edges of their seats, Brian Crowe moved into the explanation of his third theory of liability—that the defendant's actions were the proximate cause of the death of Jim Fasules.

"I've tried to summarize for you the varying testimony as to the accident itself. The judge will submit to you instructions on three theories. One was the negligence of Wolfe, for which Needham is liable. Two is the negligence of Thompson, for which Needham is liable. And the third is under the doctrine of what is called liability in tort.

"Judge Kocoras will give you the law that will say [that] if you decide that it is more probably true than not that the Chilko River is inherently dangerous and that the inherently dangerous nature of that river was a proximate cause of the injuries and death of Jim Fasules, then Needham is liable.

"And what is proximate cause? Judge Kocoras will define it for you. Judge Kocoras, I believe, will tell you that proximate cause is that which in the natural or probable sequence of events produced the injury complained of. The judge will say it need not be the last or even the nearest cause as long as it combines with some other factor to cause the injuries. Was defendant's negligence a proximate cause? Let's run through the accident and see.

"First of all, the raft is moving down the river, and Mr. Madsen told us that the raft was 200 to 225 yards from the rock. Madsen yells out to Thompson, 'The rock!' And there is no response at all from Thompson. Twice Madsen yells to Thompson. The raft proceeds to the rock and punches right through that layer of water that you saw in the diagram—the pillow of water that generally pushes a raft away from a rock. And why did the raft punch through? It was not maneuverable. There were too many men in the boat. There was too much inertia, and they couldn't respond to the high-side instruction.

"You'll recall that one of the instructions that was supposed to be given by Mr. Thompson was, 'If we're about to hit a rock, I'm going to yell, "High side!" And when I yell, "High side!," you must get everyone to that part of the boat and straighten it out.' There was no high-side instruction. And you'll see the contemporaneous notes that Collins made, which said, 'No instruction, no high side.' No high side until after that raft punches through that boundary layer and strikes that rock.

"Proximate cause? Indeed it was. The raft flips, and the men fall out. Collins stays aboard. The men all fall into the water. At this point, Collins spots Fasules within a few seconds. He says Fasules is right next to him. Can he help Fasules out? No. Collins is not aware of the throw rope, and he hasn't been instructed by Thompson on how to use a throw rope. Collins hasn't been instructed on how to pull Fasules into the raft.

"And you remember that our expert Mr. Bechdel said that a 125-pound woman, once you instruct her, can do it easily. You put your hands underneath the arms of the life vest, and you lift the person right up. Collins didn't know how to do it, and he tears the life jacket almost right off of Fasules's body. Fasules doesn't have a wetsuit or more flotation to help him out because he hasn't been given that either. And Collins has to let him go. And down the stream he goes, and he's found 25 miles later, dead.

"How about the safety kayak? We showed you where the road comes most close to the Chilko River, and there is a spot where there could be a safety kayaker. The safety kayaker could go out, get Fasules, come back, and then go out and get somebody else. But there was no safety kayaker.

"There could have been somebody there with a throw rope. There were other people helping out on that trip that could have had throw ropes, but Thompson didn't provide that either. So there was nobody to throw a throw rope to Fasules either. And worst of all, there was no second raft coming along to pick Fasules and others out of the water. All of the things that Thompson and Wolfe did were the proximate cause of that accident."

Crowe then went on to contradict Thompson's blockbuster testimony that he had pulled Jim Fasules out of the river shortly after the raft had capsized.

"But we do have some conflicting testimony. You will recall that the last two days of this trial, you heard from the defendant for the first time that Thompson rescued Fasules. You never heard that in the defendant's opening statement. You never heard about it when they cross-examined Les Bechdel.

"Did that happen? Well, let's think about that for a minute. In the Royal Canadian Mounted Police statement, Thompson said, 'I helped a passenger to shore.' But not to shore. Whomever Thompson helped, he left him standing waist deep in that cold water. Was it Fasules? I don't know, and I really don't care. Collins, however, gives an inconsistent statement. Collins says that 'I saw Jim within seconds, and I was pulling him into the raft.'

"Well, who was the man floating down the river? Could it have been the 65-year-old O'Reilly? Let's see. You're going to have a statement in evidence which you can read, and it's a statement of Mr. Morrison. Here is what Morrison says:

> Well, as I crawled out and I pulled myself out on the rocks, and I knew that I was onshore. Then I looked over, looked back behind me, and saw Dick O'Reilly go by. And he was floating, and he was on his back. But he was also moaning "Help me, help me."
>
> And it wasn't a strong "Help, help, help." It was a real moan. Then I kind of thought that he wouldn't make it. I knew that it was pretty serious that he was hurt. And then I saw that Jack Collins was still in the boat, but the boat was below me.
>
> And as I climbed out of the water and looked over on the other side, I could see Ron Thompson by that time. And he had already climbed out of the canyon on the top and was on the road. He had just reached the top and was on the road ready to run to camp, which also sort of kind of confirmed my guess of how long I was in the water because, you know, it takes a while to climb up.

"Someone was in the rapids, and he's disoriented. It could have been O'Reilly. I don't know. Could it have been Fasules? I don't know, and it doesn't matter. Because even if it was Jim Fasules, what we have is Thompson leaving a man waist-deep in the cold waters of the Chilko River.

"Thompson runs down where Zeikel is and tells him [to] take care of the men on the road. And then Thompson runs to the road and never comes back again until he gets the raft and comes down the river and picks up Miles and Morrison here and Al Wolfe, who is over here.

"Is Thompson a savior? I certainly wouldn't call Thompson a savior. And if it was Fasules that Thompson put there on the shore in waist-deep water, what difference does it make? It doesn't change the fact that the raft flipped because of Thompson's negligence. It doesn't change the fact that Fasules could have been saved if it hadn't been for Thompson's negligence.

Crowe next sought to defuse the conclusions of the Royal Canadian Mounted Police in their investigation of the accident.

"You received into evidence a judgment of inquiry. And what did the judgment of inquiry say? It said that the death of James Fasules was caused by drowning and multiple traumatic bruises as other contributing causes. In the box they marked here as to classification of events, it is marked as an accident.

"And Constable Lawrence Wiltshire told us that [an] accident does not mean that there is not civil negligence and does not mean that another court shouldn't investigate and look at civil negligence. And that's what we're doing here today. And what did the judgment of inquiry say as to the cause of the accident? Number one, no helmets; number two, no pickup points; number three, no thermal clothing, no wetsuits; and number four, no rescue plan, only one raft, and no safety kayak. The judgment of inquiry contained all of the things that the standard of care talked about.

"But these defendants have waved in front of you the fact that they found that the safety instructions of Thompson were adequate. All the coroner did was ask Thompson if he gave safety instructions, and Thompson said, 'I did.' If the coroner had looked at the statements of all the survivors, he would have seen that either no safety instructions were given or that all the men were told was to hang onto the boat.

"So when the coroner's report talks about adequate safety instructions, ask yourself what the basis of it is. How would the witnesses know what a proper safety instruction was? There is probably only one man that did, and of course he was the most experienced whitewater rafter in the group.

Crowe moved into the testimony of the standard of care of Canadian outfitters.

"There was a lot of testimony about a standard of care in this case. Was there a standard of care in British Columbia on August 1, 1987? Sure there was. Do you remember the 1979 Frasier accident where men died? Who testified there? Dan Culver said, 'Well, two rafts had a measure of safety.' He said that in 1979 before a coroner's inquest looking into the death of three boys. But he had the nerve to sit in this courtroom and look you in the eye and tell you that two rafts had nothing to do with this accident, and he wouldn't even necessarily recommend it.

"Jim Lavalley said that everyone in British Columbia was aware of the 1979 accident. Thompson is the only guy that runs one-boat trips on the Chilko. What did John McAlpine say? He said, 'I much prefer to go down in two boats. I don't want to go down in one. I only want to put six people in the raft.' And that's Thompson own man, who has been a rafter for five years.

"Lavalley said that he always ran two or more rafts. Culver's old company ran two or more rafts. And seven other outfitters who ran the Lava Canyon always took two rafts. Thompson is the only one-raft person. In the 1983 book *Rescue for River Runners*, what did that show? 'Two rafts.' In the 1984 rafting book *A Guide to Safety in British Columbia*, what does it say? 'Never raft alone.' Of course, Mr. Culver said, 'That applied to me, not to him.' There it is all over British Columbia in 1984: 'Never raft alone.' McGinnis's book *The Class V Briefing* says, 'Never raft alone.' Bechdel's testimony is, 'Never raft alone.'

"And it was known in British Columbia to wear helmets and wetsuits. They were already in use in Lava Canyon. Lavalley offered wetsuits. The helmets were primarily used in eastern Canada. McGinnis required helmets. And do you remember the 1983 University of Calgary video? It recommended helmets.

"Warnings and instructions? I ask you to think what Bechdel's testimony was and what was required by the sparse 1981 regulations that came about because of the financial interests of these men. The judge will instruct you should you consider whether those have been violated and if they had to do with the failure to warn."

Crowe discussed next an important and controversial legal topic—assumption of the risk.

"Ladies and gentlemen, there is no doubt about the fact that the negligence of these men violated standards of care in British Columbia. They were negligent, and Needham is liable for it. These defendants will stand before you today and will say that Jim Fasules assumed the risk of his own injury. Let me read to you an instruction dealing with assumption of risk that I believe His Honor Judge Kocoras will give you. The judge will tell you that the defendant has raised the affirmative defense that the decedent assumed the risk of the injuries from a danger which the plaintiff claims caused his injury.

"To prove this defense, the judge will say, the defendant has the burden of proving each of the following propositions: First, that the defendant and the decedent had an agreement under which the plaintiff was to participate in activities which exposed him to the danger that resulted in his death. Second, that the plaintiff had actual and full knowledge of the specific dangers, including the defendant's negligence, if any, and understood and appreciated the nature and extent of the risk. Third, that despite the awareness of the danger, the plaintiff deliberately and unreasonably exposed himself to this danger by a deliberate, voluntary act amounting to a considered choice. And fourth, that this danger was the cause of the plaintiff's death. Each of those propositions must be proven.

"Have they been? Let's look at the evidence in this case. As to assumption of risk, Mr. Fasules never whitewater rafted before. Two, no one ever said to him, 'You could be seriously injured or die.' Three, no one described the real hazards of rafting the Chilko River. Four, Fasules never saw the rapids in Lava Canyon. And they could have taken him right there and told him, 'Take a look at that.' All he was told was, 'Talk to Gene.'

"Or, if you want to believe Wolfe, he either told Fasules, 'Wild and woolly,' or he told him, 'The best 45 minutes.' Or did he tell him he could get cold and wet? 'When we got back Thursday,' Mr. Wolfe says, 'I was with Stuart Sharpe, and we told Jim that he could get cold and wet.' Couldn't he have been with Zeikel or Miles? No. He had to be with Stuart Sharpe, another dead man. He said somewhere in the airport, people were talking about big holes and about Class IV and Class V rapids.

"As Mr. Fasules was about to get in the raft, Al Wolfe testified that he said, 'This is going to be the thrill of your life, Jim' and that Jim looked at him and smiled. Why did he tell you that? Because he knows his lawyers want to stand up here and talk about assumption of risk.

"Madsen told us that Fasules came in the middle or the end of the conversation, and he doesn't know what Fasules heard. And even if he heard something about holes and Class IV rapids, Madsen didn't know what the classifications meant. And Madsen had actually been on whitewater before.

"Ladies and gentlemen, Collins told us that he never knew the danger of the Chilko River, and if he had, he never could have come on the trip. Lavalley said he never knew how dangerous it was until after the accident. And most telling of all, Ron Thompson says that he went down that river 208 times and that he never knew what a slim chance of survival you would have if you fell out of the raft in the Lava Canyon. Does familiarity breed contempt for the river? I don't know, but I do know that Jim Fasules never assumed the risk of his injuries, death, or the negligence of these defendants. And he did not deliberately expose himself to its dangers.

"Secondly, the defendant has another defense. The defendant has the defense that is called an act of God. The defendants are going to tell you that God, that nature, caused this. That's going to be their second defense—that somehow that rock protruded out of that river, and just the raft was there at the wrong time in the wrong place, and that this huge, unexpected wave washed that raft up against that rock. It was just an accident—it was just an act of God—and just let it go and forget about it. Well, God had nothing to do with this accident, and nature had nothing to do with this accident. This accident was caused by the negligence of Wolfe, and it was caused by the negligence of Thompson. That will be their two defenses, ladies and gentlemen."

As he wrapped up his final remarks, Brian Crowe seemed confident that he had been successful in convincing the jury of the defendant's negligence. He now had to move on to damages and, at least in his mind, seal the deal.

"I suppose the most difficult decision you're going to have in this case is a question of damages. I respectfully submit to you that I don't think liability is an issue, but damages are. And it's a hard job, and it's one that you have to do. It's one you took an oath on. And it's going to be solely and strictly your decision. You're going to be given only a few guidelines. You will be given an instruction by the court as to the elements of damages in the evidence. And the judge will give you a form of a verdict which will say that you are to consider the loss of services and society suffered by Lenore Fasules. What is the loss of services, and what is the loss of society of Lenore Fasules?

"The judge will tell you that the loss of services and society includes love and affection. It includes care. It includes attention. It includes comfort and protection. It includes companionship, and it includes friendship. What's Lenore's loss of love? I don't know. After 39 years, I think she's used to, in the middle of night, reaching over to someone who now isn't there. The affection, the kiss on the forehead by which she says, 'Jim, I'm yours, and, Jim, you're mine until death do us part.' And that's taken away, and that's part of her loss of consortium. It's part of her loss of affection.

"The loss of care. 'Lenore does your tooth hurt, back still hurt, your hand still hurt?' 'Lenore, why don't you go to a doctor?' 'Do you think, Lenore, maybe you ought to go to a dentist?' 'Lenore, it's just the weather. Don't worry about it.' And that's gone, and there will be no one to give her that anymore. And that's part of her loss of services and society.

"And the loss of comfort. It's a loss of someone being able to hold, hug you when you're depressed, to squeeze your hand when you're worried, do nothing more but just sit there and be quite with you. And the loneliness. The times that you used to hear sounds in the house, and you never worried about those sounds because Jim was there. And now in the loneliness of that house those sounds become ominous.

"Those are all part of her loss for the rest of her life. Did she lose a friend and a companion? She sure did. Jim was the friend and the companion, the affection and the love that she doesn't have anymore. No one to go to China with or take other trips with and stand by the Chinese wall. And there is no one like Jim to go fishing with again and no one to say, 'Hey, Jim, you know what the grandchildren are doing, little Sandy and little Megan?' Not to be able to talk about what they did or how maybe son Jim screwed up or Nancy got something good in life and not be able to share these things with her husband. And for the rest of her life, Lenore will have to do without that.

"What is the value of Lenore's loss of services and society? I invite Mr. Swindal when he comes up here to tell you what he believes the value of the loss of Jim to Lenore is. I respectfully submit to you that you consider that loss of services and society to be $1,500,000.

"The judge will then instruct you that you are to consider the loss of services and society of Nancy Fasules. What is the loss of her father to Nancy, the girl who would never do what her dad said, who wouldn't stay in college, who finally did at his urging, who wouldn't go into advertising at the urging and for years went on to be a lyricist. And yet her dad cared about her, and she knew that her dad cared. And she'd come to his home at Christmas and Easter. And she won't be able to visit him there anymore.

"And there were times, of course, that he'd stop to see her and encourage her. And she will be waiting for the day—and it will never come—when she can says, 'Hey, Dad, I finally got that big hit.' But most of all, the day will come when she'll get married, and there won't be a dad to walk her down the aisle and hold her hand and give her in marriage. The judge will then instruct you as to the loss of services. And I would say to you—and it's up to you—that you would consider for the loss of services and society Nancy Fasules to be awarded the sum of $500,000.

"As to the loss of services and society for the son James Fasules, Jim has lost a fishing partner. He's lost a companion; he's lost a friend. He's lost someone to say, 'Hey, doctor, I'm proud of you.' And he's lost a babysitter for these youngsters, and he's lost the joy in his father's face as he looks at these kids. He's lost all of that. There will be no more letters to Santa Claus. And I suggest to you that you award Jim Fasules the sum of $500,000 for his loss of services and society.

"As to son Gary Fasules, he stands with his mom and dad at the Chinese wall not because he went on the trip with them but because he was there for business. Do you remember what he said? 'I didn't want to go.' And his dad said, 'Do it, Gary. Do it. Get in there. Do that business.' And Gary said, 'It was the greatest thing I ever did.' His dad was his business adviser. Things that Gary did in business he relied upon his dad on. And he won't have his dad to rely on anymore. And what did Al Wolfe say that Gary said to him the last day? I suggest that you return a verdict on behalf of Gary Fasules in the sum of $500,000.

"Finally, the judge is going to instruct you as to the economic or the pecuniary loss to the estate of James Fasules. What is it? You will recall testimony in this case as to lost earnings of James Fasules. You will be given a jury instruction that says there are tables of mortality giving the average life expectancy of how long people live. Now, Jim's mom from Germany and his dad from Greece lived to be well in their nineties. But let's stay with the tables of mortality. There was the testimony about the Nevada Mining stock, the consulting fee. Two million dollars was to be split between him and the doctor. He would have also earned $150,000, and his family could have enjoyed that had it not been for this tragedy. There was 10 years of teaching at the University of Reno at $70,000 per year, which included salary and benefits of $700,000. There was $15,000 cash per year for five years for consulting from ValuCom. That was $75,000. And there was other consulting services at $1,000 per day for 10 days per year over the next 10 years with the Management Analysis Center, which is of $100,000. The total comes to $1,025,000. I would ask—and it is your decision—that for economic loss to the estate that you award a sum of $1 million.

"And finally, there is the pain and suffering of Jim Fasules. Pain and suffering is both mental and physical. As to the physical pain, I don't want to spend much time on that. But I think we can try to imagine what it's like when our vessels and our organs are violated by the river and we can't breathe. I think we can imagine what the pain had to be like going down the Chilko River. And Madsen told us—everyone has told us they were yelling. And Madsen told us that his kidneys were bruised, and his ribs were broken. And there were the faces of the men that weren't even recognizable. They couldn't be identified. You saw the huge gash down Fasules's head. It's physical pain and suffering.

"But Jim's mental pain and suffering was far worse. If Collins is right—and I believe he is—then Jim Fasules suffered the fear of dying before Collins brought him into the raft. And he suffered the fear of dying after Collins had to let him go. And if Mr. Thompson is right, then he suffered the fear of dying three times. He suffered the fear of dying as someone pulled him by the hand and left him waist high in the water, and he suffered the fear of dying before Collins brought him in the raft. And he suffered the fear of dying as he was sucked down the Chilko River and he was found 50 miles away. What do you think about when you're dying? I don't know. But I think at least your mind rolls over what you had and what you don't have anymore. I think a mind has to think about your wife. It's got to think about your children, and it's got about the grandchildren that you have, that you won't have, and the losses that they will suffer. And the losses that you suffer and any one of them suffers is the loss of each other, and it is four times greater.

"This man should not have died in the Chilko River. He shouldn't have suffered because another man wanted thrills, another man wanted to go down that Chilko River to touch the face of death and share that experience with other men so there would be a bonding. He never should have brought that 63-year-old Jim Fasules on that trip. And I ask that you award a verdict for Mr. Fasules for his conscious pain and suffering of $1 million. I would suggest to you the total sum of $5 million. You may think it's too much, or you may think it's too little. But the fact remains that you are the conscience of the community in which you live. Whatever you do here today, Mrs. Fasules will be content with and your community will be content with. I ask that you return a verdict for Mrs. Fasules, for her children, and for the estate.

"Thank you for your time and for your attention."

# Chapter Fourteen

Now that Crowe had made his closing argument, Bill Swindal had the responsibility of convincing the jury that Needham was not liable for the drowning of Jim Fasules. Swindal was aware of the immensity of the task before him.

Swindal approached the jury with the same earnest demeanor that had characterized his time before the court.

"Good afternoon, ladies and gentlemen. Is it a tragedy that this accident happened? Yes. Is it a tragedy that five men died? Absolutely. But we're not here to decide if it was a tragedy. We're here to decide whether DDB Needham is responsible for the loss of James Fasules. I submit to you that the evidence is that the company is not.

"Whitewater rafting is a recreational and sporting activity that is engaged in by all kinds of people. You heard evidence that on average, over 2 million people engage in this type of recreational sporting activity each year in the United States alone. In British Columbia, it was no different. People have been rafting the Chilko River through Lava Canyon commercially for over 13 years prior to August 1, 1987, without a single accident.

"Ron Thompson had been operating his business on the Chilko River for those same 13 years with an exemplary safety record. No one had been injured. There were over 200 trips through Lava Canyon without an incident. You've heard that Ron Thompson carried 70 percent of the commercial traffic through Lava Canyon. No one who knew or regulated the commercial rafting business in British Columbia has come into this courtroom to say anything other than that Ron Thompson was the most experienced, qualified guide on the Chilko River on and before August 1, 1987. All the operators and guides in British Columbia have shown a long proven record of safety. This is the only rafting accident on the Chilko River.

"Ladies and gentlemen, the record of performance and activity on the Chilko River is direct, uncontroverted evidence that commercial river rafting through Lava Canyon was not, and is not, inherently dangerous. To claim otherwise, as Mr. Crowe does, is to ignore the actual history and track record of Ron Thompson and the rafters through Lava Canyon. To equate this proven safety record in Lava Canyon with an inherently dangerous activity constitutes unsubstantiated exaggeration and overreaching.

"Plaintiffs ask you to believe that this case is about power and machismo, with Al Wolfe leading the charge like Rambo through the rain forest of Southeast Asia. Ladies and gentlemen, it would be easier to track a field mouse through the forest than to find proof of that in this case. Again, unsubstantiated exaggeration. You heard Al Wolfe, and you saw him testify in this case. You be the judges if that was Rambo.

"As I told you in the opening statement, you must decide whether Al Wolfe did something wrong that caused the death of Jim Fasules without resorting to the sympathy and emotional clouds that Mr. Crowe brings to this case to drape over the real facts. What did Al Wolfe do in this case? He organized the trip. No doubt about it. He selected the most qualified and experienced guide on the Chilko River he could find.

"All of the experts in this case, including Mr. Bechdel, agreed that an organizer and the participants on a trip have a right to rely on the guide. Mr. Bechdel called him 'the river professional.' We all know what professionals are—doctors, lawyers, accountants, engineers, musicians, lawyers, judges, businessmen, precision tool workers, managers. There are all kinds of professions. And we rely on them in every part of our life. Al Wolfe asked James Fasules if he would like to go on a trip where there would be great fishing and 45 minutes of whitewater on a wild and woolly river.

"Al Wolfe extended an invitation. Al Wolfe had no knowledge of any accidents or safety problems on the Chilko River beyond those risks that are obvious to all of us. You will be instructed that Al Wolfe had a duty to warn Fasules of dangers that were not open and obvious to Fasules but were known to Al Wolfe. The risks of whitewater rafting were open and obvious to James Fasules. Whitewater—that's not a swimming pool. It means something more than a lazy stroll down the

Lincoln Park lagoon. And there is no proof in this case that Al Wolfe knew any more of the dangers of the Chilko River than those that are open and obvious to everyone. In fact, ladies and gentlemen, all of the experts who came here from British Columbia to talk about this accident said that no one knew of the problems that were encountered on August 1, 1987.

"You've heard a lot about James Fasules in this case. We've learned to know the man. We've learned that James Fasules was a very intelligent and sophisticated businessman. We've learned that James Fasules was an independent thinker who made judgments and decisions for himself. Mr. Crowe described James Fasules as a 'Class A, aggressive-type person, an organized, self-confident, aggressive person.' Those who worked with him agreed. And Mr. Fasules's close personal friend and business associate described James Fasules as 'a very bright and intelligent man with an organized and inquisitive mind.' James Fasules was a man who knew what he wanted to do and did it. He made his own decisions, and no one made those for him.

"The evidence is also that James Fasules knew the risks of water, moving water, whitewater. He knew the natural and obvious characteristics of whitewater and its danger. He knew what might happen. He may not have known all the technical terms, the size of the waves, the size of the logs, and the other elements that Mr. Crowe talked about in his argument. But he knew the risks. He had been around water all of his life.

"Even the plaintiff's expert Bechdel admitted that James Fasules knew what whitewater rafting included. It included the possibility of drowning if he fell out of that raft. James Fasules knew this was a vigorous whitewater rafting trip. He knew it was on a wild and woolly river. He knew what the risks and dangers were, and he eagerly accepted that invitation and decided to go.

"James Fasules told Earl Madsen that he wouldn't have missed this trip for anything. He told Earl Madsen he would be rafting on Saturday. He heard the descriptions and the discussions about this river at the Vancouver airport twice on Thursday, once at that campfire that evening, and again on Saturday. He was also knew that if he didn't want to raft—he was told on Thursday and again on Saturday—there were vans. 'If you don't want to get in the raft and go, then take the van.' He knew that. But no. You heard Mr. Madsen say he decided to get in the raft. In fact, he wanted to sit in the front. Like all of the other decisions he made in his life, James Fasules knew what he wanted, and he made that decision. He assumed those risks. There is no credible evidence that James Fasules did not know what he was doing, and there is no evidence that anyone forced him to raft.

"Now, the evidence in this trial has proven that there is a substantial and important difference between an organizer and a guide and what their roles are. There has been no dispute by the expert witnesses as to the role and duties of the river guide. All of them testified that the guide is in total and compete charge of the rafting trip. He's the captain of that ship. And it's only the guide who makes the decisions of when to raft, what equipment to us, how to raft. And he alone gives the safety instructions. The organizer doesn't have any of those duties or responsibilities."

Bill Swindal walked closer to the jury box, and his tone of voice suddenly changed to one of righteous indignation.

"To do what Mr. Crowe has asked you to do in reaching your verdict, you must determine that all of the witnesses who were there on August 1, 1987—Earl Madsen, Jack Collins, Art Zeikel, Joe Morrison, Al Wolfe, Mike Miles, and Ron Thompson—are liars. And that all of the witnesses who know and regulated commercial river rafting in British Columbia are wrong and that you shouldn't believe them.

"Further, to go along with Mr. Crowe's theory, you have to determine that the British Columbia court of inquiry is not only incompetent but untruthful and that their investigation and the Mounties' investigation is hogwash. To reach the verdict that Mr. Crowe is urging on you, you must determine that Al Wolfe got into that raft with his friends knowing that they would die when they fell out. How does Mr. Crowe explain why Al got into that raft if he knew it was unsafe? He can't.

"To reach the decision that Mr. Crowe urges, you then have to believe only Les Bechdel. Who is Les Bechdel, and what is his knowledge and experience in rafting in British Columbia prior to August 1, 1987? Les Bechdel is the plaintiff's hired gun. He is the only person in this entire trial to put blame on DDB Needham or anybody else. Yet he admits that he has absolutely no experience on the Chilko River. He'd never even seen it until July of 1989, and then he went down it in a kayak.

"He has no credible knowledge or experience about the Chilko River or commercial rafting in British Columbia as it existed on August 1, 1987. He nevertheless came into this courtroom and for nearly two days sat on that stand and told you well that he knew more about commercial rafting in British Columbia than anybody else. He knew more than the Royal Canadian Mounted Police; he knew more than the British Columbia court of inquiry; he knew more about the people who were running trips for 13 years in British Columbia. But he knew. In fact, I think he told you that *he* was the standard of care in British Columbia.

"That's simply incredible, ladies and gentlemen. It's just more exaggeration and overreaching that anybody like Les Bechdel could come into this courtroom and profess to be so all-knowing and omnipotent and yet have so little to back it up. However, even Les Bechdel admitted that the outfitter is in total charge of the trip, not the organizer. Bechdel likes to use organizers. It helps him. They do the nitty-gritty, and he doesn't have to worry about that. He said that he has his customers sign a form where they acknowledge in writing that they knew what James Fasules knew—that things go wrong on trips; that there are inherent risks in whitewater rafting; and that even the most careful person cannot avoid it."

Bill Swindal began concluding his final remarks, and he knew it would be his last opportunity to convince the jury that his client had acted responsibly and should bear no responsibility for the untimely and inexplicable death of a very decent man named Jim Fasules.

"At the end of our argument, I believe Judge Kocoras will instruct you that the mere fact that an accident happened does not permit the jury to draw the inference that the accident must have been caused by someone's negligence. Bechdel admits that people can drown if they fall out of a boat on whitewater rafting; he admits that Ron Thompson was a certified guide with the most experience on the river; he admits that the self-bailing boat used by Ron Thompson was the safest and state of the art; he admits that as an outfitter, he himself did not use wetsuits or helmets prior to August 1, 1987; he admits the life jackets were proper; and he admits that the final and ultimate decision to board that raft belongs to the participant, James Fasules. And, lastly, he admits that James Fasules knew the natural characteristics of whitewater.

"Ron Thompson came into the courtroom. He took his oath, and he said that he and he alone was in charge of this trip. He made the decisions. No one told him to do anything, and no one pressured him to do anything. He made those decisions.

"The evidence here, ladies and gentlemen, has proven that DDB Needham did nothing wrong to cause the death of James Fasules. They retained the most qualified, experienced, and competent guide on the Chilko River to run this trip. And everybody who knew the commercial rafting business in British Columbia has testified that this guide acted in conformity with the existing standards of care. We didn't have any Monday morning quarterbacks in this trial.

"This evidence has proven that the Chilko River through Lava Canyon has been rafted commercially on a continuous and regular basis for 13 years prior to this accident without an injury. The evidence proves it to be not inherently dangerous. Notwithstanding the care and efforts of DDB Needham in setting up this trip and finding the most competent guide the tragic accident happened. It could have just as easily happened to Al Wolfe. We submit, ladies and gentlemen, that the evidence has proven that James Fasules knew what he was doing when he said, 'Yes. I want to go on this trip. I wouldn't miss it for the world.' He assumed those risks.

"I told you in opening statement that James Fasules was a good man, a good father, and a good husband. And you've heard nothing to contradict it during the entire course of this trial because it's true. When you peel away all the hyperbole, all the exaggeration and overreaching, and all the emotion and sympathy that Mr. Crowe likes to bring into this case—when you pull out all those extraneous matters—DDB Needham is *not* responsible for the death of James Fasules. Your common sense and your knowledge of the ordinary affairs of life tell you that. If it weren't true, ladies and gentlemen, why would Al Wolfe put himself in that raft?

"Now, I believe the court will instruct you at the end of the case that if you find for DDB Needham on the issue of liability, you won't have to talk about damages. But I would be remiss in my job if I didn't talk about damages with you briefly. Mr. Crowe has requested $5 million. I'd like Mr. Crowe to explain to you what that amount of money does when it's put into a bank. It probably generates $400,000 a year forever.

And at some time between now and the end of forever, that $5 million is still there.

"Your verdict must be reasonable and not based on speculation or conjecture or wishes. Have Mr. Crowe identify for you any actual real income that was being earned by Mr. Fasules at the time of his death. He was retired and wanted to stay retired. He had already turned down job offers. Mr. Crowe had some real big numbers up there about Valu-Com, but it was all wish list on the compensation. And it's incredible that someone who taught two two-week seminars would be raised to the level of dean of the department overnight. He had already turned down full-time jobs. I suggest that if damages are to be awarded in this case, they have to be reasonable and real—not made out of conjecture, wish, and hope.

"Ladies and gentlemen, I ask that your verdict be for the defendant. I too would like to thank you on behalf of my client for the time and perseverance you've put into this trial. It is truly appreciated."

# Epilogue

When all was said and done, the jury awarded Mrs. Fasules $1 million for an inexplicable accident involving a highly experienced guide with a perfect safety record and full releases of liability from all the passengers on the trip.

Jury verdicts are always curious things. And because juries are comprised of individuals, the limitations of humanity are on full display. A widow asking to be compensated for the loss of her husband is difficult to resist, especially when the jury can rationalize that a distant insurance company will be forced to pay the judgment with funds that will never be missed.

The small-town rafting outfitter, which had not been sued, was reluctant to point an accusing finger at the individual who organized the corporate outing—an avid rafting enthusiast himself—even though that individual may have overstepped the boundaries of safety when insisting that everyone in his group travel together in the name of camaraderie and team building, in spite of the possibility of an overloaded boat.

No one wants to acknowledge the nasty rumor that one of the boaters who drowned, perhaps a little heavyset and not particularly athletic, lost his balance and fell into the outfitter, causing him to miss an oar stroke and veer sideways into the powerful hydraulic.

Certainly no one wants to bring up the pesky issue that before the trip all of the participants signed a release and an acknowledgment of risk.

And finally, no wants to admit that whitewater rafting will always contain elements of unpredictability or that otherwise it would amount to a glorified amusement park ride.

In the end, a wild river is a force of nature that can be approached with caution and competence but one that can never be completely tamed.

# Index

respiratory gas reflex, 120
risk: assumption of, 12, 55, 70, 132–
    33, 134; management, 76; release-
    and-assumption-of-the-risk form,
    27, 36, 37
River Outfitters Association of
    British Columbia (ROABC), 99,
    102, 112
*River Rescue* (Ray), 75
ROABC. *See* River Outfitters
    Association of British Columbia
rope-throwing and throw ropes, 8,
    10, 36, 65, 76, 77, 103, 127
Royal Canadian Mounted Police, 11,
    99, 117, 119, 130, 143

safety: "accepted safety standard,"
    106; concerns, 49; gear, 80;
    instructions, 8, 36, 59, 65, 73, 108,
    131; kayaks, 8, 12, 78, 80, 107,
    127, 129; plan, 76; precautions,
    113–14, 115; procedures,
    36; record, 85, 99, 140, 147;
    regulations, 103; talks, 108, 114
Salmon River: Main Fork of, 75, 79,
    81; Middle Fork of, 68, 75
self-rescue, 65, 74, 115, 117
Selway River, 3, 52, 68, 69, 124
services, loss of, 135–36
Sharpe, Stuart, x, xi, 6–7, 10, 14, 16,
    46, 133; body recovery of, 11, 47;
    release-and-assumption-of-the-
    risk form and, 27
Sobek (adventure-travel
    consolidator), 15, 22
society, loss of, 135–36
Sonora, California, 111
standards and conditions, written,
    99–103
standards of care, 112, 132–33, 144
steelhead trout, 5, 17

subpoenas, 89
suffering, 12, 137
swift-water rescue, 117
Swindal, Bill, 22–23, 135–36, 139,
    142; Bechdel and, 81–83, 85–87;
    jury introductions by, 20; Madsen
    and, 55–61, 63–64; opening
    statement by, 19; sincerity of, 25;
    Wolfe and, 67–74
swing weight phenomenon, 76

tables of mortality, 137
Taseko junction, 24, 63, 69, 77, 95,
    117
temperature, of water, 100
Thompson, Ron, x, xi, 10, 30–31, 39,
    51–52, 126–34, 139; Bechdel on,
    75–77; coroner on, 25–26, 131;
    Davy and, 89–97, 103; dismissal
    as witness, 96; equipment and,
    29; experience of, ix, 22, 118;
    high-side command and, 41;
    Lavalley on, 111–17; liability
    and, 40; life jackets and, 29, 59,
    65, 73, 101, 115; Madsen and,
    36, 59–60, 64–65; McAlpine
    on, 7, 21; negligence and, 9, 12,
    36, 41, 79, 128, 131, 134; safety
    instructions and, 8, 36, 48, 108;
    safety kayaks and, 78; safety
    record and, 85; safety regulations
    and, 103; standards of care and,
    104; Wolfe and, 4, 6–7, 15, 22,
    32, 68–70, 72–74, 83, 125
Thompson River, 112
throw ropes and rope-throwing, 8,
    10, 36, 65, 76, 77, 103, 127
trial by jury, 19
trout, steelhead, 5, 17

United States, 139

# About the Author

**Cecil Kuhne** is particularly qualified to tell the riveting adventure story of *The White Mile Trial*, as he is both an experienced whitewater rafting guide and an attorney. On the adventure side, he is the author of 10 books on river running, and most recently, he is the author of *River Master: John Wesley Powell's Legendary Exploration of the Colorado River and Grand Canyon*. He has also edited five popular adventure-travel anthologies. On the legal side, he is the author of 23 books on litigation published by the American Bar Association, including *Adventure Law*. In addition to practicing law with one of the largest law firms in the world, he works part-time as a rafting guide on the Colorado River in the Grand Canyon.